THE
DRUID MAGIC
Handbook

Ritual Magic Rooted
in the Living Earth

John Michael Greer

Foreword by David Spangler

WEISERBOOKS
San Francisco, CA / Newburyport, MA

First published in 2007 by
Red Wheel/Weiser, LLC
With offices at:
665 Third Street, Suite 400
San Francisco, CA 94107
www.redwheelweiser.com

Library of Congress Cataloging-in-Publication Data
Greer, John Michael.
  The Druid magic handbook : ritual magic rooted in the living earth / John
Michael Greer ; foreword by David Spangler.
      p. cm.
  Includes bibliographical references and index.
  ISBN 978-1-57863-397-5 (alk. paper)
  1. Druids and druidism. 2. Magic, Celtic. I. Title.
  BL910.G746 2007
  299'.16133--dc22
                                    2007033118

Cover and text design by Donna Linden
Typeset in Centaur and Perpetua
Cover photograph © Larry Brownstein/Getty Images
Oak tree illustration © Rich Harris/iStockphoto

Printed in the United States of America

10 9 8 7 6 5 4 3

CONTENTS

FOREWORD

When, in the early '70s, I was a codirector of the Findhorn Foundation Community, an international spiritual center in the north of Scotland, I had the pleasure of knowing and working with Robert Ogilvy Crombie (or ROC, as he was known by his friends). He was a lively, gentle, and loving elderly Scot who was a Hermetic magician. Though he lived in Edinburgh, he was a frequent visitor to the community and an integral part of its spiritual life. Findhorn is best known around the world for its contact with the inner kingdoms of nature—the spiritual intelligences behind all growing things. Part of this contact was made by Dorothy Maclean, one of the three founders of the community, whose specialty was communication with the "devas" or angels of various plant species. It was ROC, though, who had contact and communication with the elemental forces of nature, the Nature Spirits. This contact was his most public contribution, but behind the scenes, he had a special role as the community's guardian. It was in this regard that I came to know and respect his magical skills and knowledge.

For his ceremonial work, ROC said he used the tradition originating with the fabled Order of the Golden Dawn, the famous magical lodge established in England in the late 1880s that became the renewing, driving force behind so much of the occultism and magic of the twentieth century. However, his training was something of a mystery. A heart ailment at an early age had kept him from holding a steady job. Told by doctors to seek out isolation and quiet, he lived for many years in a cottage in an ancient forest, rather Merlin-like. It was there that he made the deep contact with the forces of nature and, I believe, based on things he told me, it was there under their tutelage that he learned the basic principles of magic, principles he later augmented by extensive study in the fields of psychology, physics, and the Hermetic writings of Western magic.

Whatever the nature of his training, ROC clothed his magic in a context of attunement to nature. Although he lived in the center of a major city, nature was supremely important to him. Indeed, although he never claimed such a thing, I often felt in his presence that I was with a Druid.

In 1973, I returned from Findhorn and Scotland to pick up my work in the United States. Before I left, I had a final conversation with ROC in which he said he felt he was one of the last practitioners of an older tradition of magic. "A new form of magic is unfolding," he said, "I can see it, but it's not for me to do. It's for you and those of your generation and the next."

These words echoed something I had been told several years earlier. From childhood on, I have had an ongoing contact with nonphysical beings. One summer, right after my graduation from high school but before I entered college, I had had a short, unexpected visit from a being who said simply, "In the future, a new form of spirituality will unfold. With it will come a new kind of magic." At the time, I had just stored this away under the "Interesting-but-I-don't-know-what-to-do-about-it" mental file. But ROC's words reawakened my alertness to new possibilities in the field of magic and spirituality.

However, although I had an interest in magic and practiced a very personal form of it that I wove out of my own inner experiences, my work and life took me in other directions. It was not for another twenty years that magic began to occupy my attention again in a serious way. By then I had begun to meet and work with modern magicians who were trained in the old methods but were transforming them through their own insights and experiences. People such as John and Caitlin Matthews, William Bloom, R. J. Stewart, and others seemed to me to be pushing at the envelope of the magical traditions and opening exciting possibilities for new directions in the magical arts. And I began my own experiments in that direction as well, exploring what I call an "incarnational magic."

Then I came across a book that sent me on an expedition to find everything that its author had written. The book was *Inside a Magical Lodge,* one of the finest and clearest books on the magical tradition and its structure that I had found. The author was John Michael Greer, the writer of the excellent book you are now holding. Soon, thanks to the wonders of the Internet and the services of *Amazon.com* (and what Renaissance mage ever had such a willing and able invisible servant to bring him knowledge?), I had everything John Michael had written and was working my way through it with a rising excitement.

For what I discovered when I read *Inside a Magical Lodge* and, subsequently, his other books was three things: a brilliant scholarly mind that was deeply knowledgeable of the history and traditions of the magical arts, the practical wisdom of an experienced practitioner of those arts, and, most important from my point of view, the inner feel of someone on the track of formulating a new kind of magic for the twenty-first century.

I decided I wanted to get to know this man. But I had no idea where he was.

This is where magic stepped in. I had been invited to speak at a summer conference in Oregon near the Columbia River Gorge, a spectacularly beautiful area. The event was held in a rural camp under the trees. Early on the morning I was to give a workshop, I stood in the main clearing looking at a large board with the day's schedule on it and saw that the other speaker of the day was John Michael Greer! Hooray! Here would be my chance to meet him. But closer inspection saw that we were teaching at the same time in different areas of the camp. I would not be able to go hear him talk after all.

I heard a sigh behind me and saw a tall, bearded, handsome fellow standing a few feet away also contemplating the schedule board.

"Conflicts?" I asked.

"Yes," he said.

"Me, too. I really wanted to hear John Michael Greer, but I'm teaching a workshop at the same time."

"Are you David Spangler?" he asked.

"Yes."

"Well, I'm John Michael Greer, and I wanted to hear you!"

If there was no magic behind this meeting, then I will eat my hat. But even magic only goes so far. We still didn't get to hear each other that day. A friend of mine did go listen to John Michael, whose talk introduced some of the themes in this book, and he consoled me by telling me—several times and at length—just how excellent John Michael had been!

Since then I have had the pleasure of making up for my loss that day, both in personal communications and visits with John Michael and in enjoying his prolificacy with books. One of his latest, *A World Full of Gods,* I am already using as a textbook in some of my classes on contemporary spirituality, and I have no doubt that I will be using this one as well.

What most attracts me to John Michael's work is that I see him as one of those who are bringing a new understanding and practice of magic into being. When because of my own inner contact and later because of ROC's words, I began to consider that new ways of working magic were going to appear, my thoughts turned toward the forms of magic. By "new magic," I thought what was meant were new forms of ritual or new ways of contacting spiritual sources of energy and power. I had to grow in my own experience to realize that this isn't what was meant at all. It's not that new forms may not appear or have not appeared; people are experimenting with magical forms and rituals all the time. But the essence of a new magic—the kind of thing ROC was talking about and I assume my inner contact was predicting— lies in a new understanding of the nature of magic itself. Not just an understanding of how to do it, but of what it is.

Magic, as John Michael eloquently points out in this book, is not some glamorous, supernatural power apart from life. It is the energies and processes of life itself. It is rooted in our connectedness with the life of the world around us, and its greatest effect is to root us and connect us even more fully. In fact, one could say that magic is the expression of our connectedness. A magician, we come to see, is not someone who stands apart and wields vast forces in some impersonal manner from a lonely mountain top. Rather he or she is a person who is immersed in the world, a participant, part of the life of nature, part of the life of humanity, at home in forests and in cities, wherever life is. To "do magic" is to serve life. It is to enhance the capacity of life, in whatever form, to be fully what it is and to become perhaps more than it might expect.

John Michael knows this point and is able to convey it in clear and compelling prose. He is not only a fine and experienced magician. He is also a blessedly fine writer. I'm envious on both counts!

In this book, John Michael is presenting a specific form of magic, namely Druid magic. The specificity is important. In our world, life manifests through forms and bodies. It possesses particularity. The raccoons that occasionally sleep in the trees in my backyard are not the same as the trees, and both are different from me. Druid magic is not the Hermetic magic of the Order of the Golden Dawn, nor is it Egyptian magic, nor Native American magic. It's important to understand and honor the differences and not attempt to make one the other. I would make a poor raccoon and an even poorer tree.

So John Michael gifts us with a powerful form based on ancient traditions. If we are Druids, we can appreciate the connectedness and depth this magical form offers us with all that we love and honor in the Druid path. If we are not Druids, we can still appreciate the spirit of connection and depth of practice this book offers and the vision it offers of holistic ways, connected ways, and collaborative ways of doing magic.

Either way, it offers us a chance to fulfill the vision of a new magic, for behind the practices and techniques John Michael offers is something I feel is more subtle and maybe more important: the idea that it isn't a new magic that is evolving but new magicians. It is magicians who understand the honor of being human but at the same time the responsibility and joy of being connected, of being part of a larger wholeness of life and serving the energies that flow through that wholeness. It is the vision of a magician who loves, indeed who is love.

The Druid path may well offer a greater opportunity to come to this place, but it is really open to any of us, whatever path we walk. For magical forms can come and go and, as ROC pointed out, will come and go, but the magical place of interconnectedness and love where we can stand in collaboration with the world is always available to us. Learning how to go to that place and stand there and be a sacred mage in service to all life: that is the new magic. Its secrets are in each of us. From that place we can step into any magical or ritual form. When we do, the magic that is forever and always in us will enliven and enlighten the magic that is potential in the form.

This is the vision that John Michael Greer offers. He is truly one of the New Magicians.

ROC would have been pleased.

David Spangler
Author of *Blessing: The Art and the Practice;
The Story Tree; Apprenticed to Spirit*

INTRODUCTION

When the founders of the Druid Revival began the long process of creating modern Druidry back in the early eighteenth
century, magic was very nearly the last thing on their minds.
Like many people of their time, they watched the birth of the
Industrial Age and the first stirrings of today's environmental crises, and they recognized that the cultural forces driving humanity apart from nature would never be able to solve
the problems humans were causing. Faced with a Hobson's
choice between dogmatic religion and materialist science,
they took a third path, drawing inspiration from the legacy
of the ancient Celtic Druids to craft a new spirituality of
nature. It never seems to have occurred to them, however,
that magic might be part of that path.

At that time, the magical traditions of the Western world
were at their lowest ebb in many centuries. Gone were the
heady days of the Renaissance, when great mages such as Para-
celsus, Cornelius Agrippa, and Giordano Bruno proclaimed
the reality of magic to the world and the occult traditions
counted as a major cultural force. The scientific revolution
put paid to all that, banishing the occult vision of a cosmos
woven together by subtle threads of power and meaning and

replacing it with Newton's universe of dead matter spinning through an infinite void. Magic still existed in the eighteenth century—never in all of human history has there been a culture without magic—but its practitioners either lived among the rural poor or belonged to an underworld of secretive magical lodges on the fringes of contemporary culture.

A few of the founders of the Druid Revival had contacts with the old magical wisdom, but those traditions played no role worth noticing in the creation of Druidry. Not until the great revival of occultism in the late nineteenth century did the first magical practices start finding their way into the Druid movement, and it took most of a century thereafter for magic to become a significant part of the modern Druid tradition. Even today, some of the more conservative Druid Revival orders will have nothing to do with magic.

Still, magic has a valid place in Druidry today. Partly, of course, the ancient Celtic Druids who provided the original inspiration for the Revival, and whose example still guides it today, had a reputation all through ancient times as first-rate magicians. Partly, the Western world's rejection of magic has much more to do with the crisis of industrial civilization than the founders of the Druid Revival ever guessed.

On another level, however, magic belongs in Druidry because the core principles of Druidry and magic are the same. Both unfold from the awareness that the world around us is a community to which we belong, not a commodity we can own. Both recognize that subtle connections weave every part of the cosmos together and offer us unexpected ways to sense and shape the flow of events. Both realize that our fate is a co-creation of our actions and the patterns of space, time, and meaning that define the world around us.

That these principles also form the foundations of ecology stands as a sign of their wider importance.

Still, magic plays a less central role in Druidry than it does in some other alternative spiritualities today. The core practices of the Druid path remain what they were in the eighteenth century: daily life lived in harmony with nature, seasonal rituals that celebrate the cycles of nature, and meditation to unveil the secrets of our own nature. Magic combines well with all of these but cannot replace any of them. Nor is magic necessarily part of every Druid's path, for many other arts—poetry, music, divination, healing, sacred geometry, and the study of ancient traditions of the sacred landscape, among others—have long been part of the Druid tradition, and each Druid chooses from these and other options in creating his or her personal approach to Druid nature spirituality.

For those who hear its call, however, magic offers possibilities that few other Druid arts can equal. Just as the banishing of magic by industrial society has deep connections with the failures of vision that put our civilization on a collision course with ecological reality, the rebirth of Druid magic has immense potential as a tool for healing the split between humanity and nature and dissolving the trance that blinds us to our oneness with the living Earth.

A Few Words about Authenticity

One of the questions I field most often as a teacher of Druidry is "Where do today's Druid teachings come from?" Most of the people who pose that question want to know if the Druid magic we practice today comes down directly from the ancient Celtic Druids, and many of them feel bitterly disappointed when they learn that the magic of the old Druids vanished forever more than a thousand years ago.

We know, as it happens, that the ancient Druids practiced magic. We know almost nothing about the magic they practiced, because all the information about the old Druids that comes from the days when they still existed amounts to ten pages of brief passages from Greek and Latin writers, most of whom never met a Druid. References in legends of Christian saints from Celtic countries and passages from Irish legends have a little more to say, but those were written centuries after the Druids died out, and how much ancient lore they contain is the subject of hot debate among scholars today. All these sources put together offer only a few fragments of Druid magic—not enough to teach anyone today how to practice authentic Druid magic.

Thus it deserves to be said up front that not one bit of today's Druid magic comes from the ancient Druids. The teachings included in this book are no exception. They trace their roots to the Druid Revival movement, and they evolved to meet the needs of people practicing Druidry in the modern world. They draw extensively on eighteenth- and nineteenth-century Welsh Druid lore, like most Revival traditions, but also draw on other sources within and beyond the Druid community.

All this counts as next thing to heresy in some circles. Saying that a tradition rooted in the Druid Revival and the Renaissance can call itself "Druid magic," for that matter, is bound to raise hackles in some corners of today's alternative spiritual scene. There are writers and teachers today who insist that the value of any system of Druid practice depends on its claim to historical authenticity. If Druid teachings don't copy the practices of the ancient Celtic Druids as exactly as possible, this argument goes, they must not be worth much.

This sort of thinking has tangled roots. Many people yearn for ways of life more richly human than the ones they find in today's industrial society. Such yearnings speak to powerful needs, but a quirk of the modern imagination leads many of those who feel the call to a better life to think they have to find it in some other culture far from ours in space or time. The ancient Celts have been targeted more than most others by this sort of thinking, and as a result you can find many books in print today that paint the Celts of the past in the colors of Utopia.

The reality is much more nuanced. Just like ours, ancient Celtic cultures had vices as well as virtues—societies that had no moral problem at all with slavery and defined people's human value based on their social class, as the ancient Celts did, make very poor candidates for Utopia by most standards—and their traditions, colorful as they may seem from a distance, aren't all that relevant to the very different realities of life in a declining industrial civilization. The Celtic heritage has been a source of inspiration for modern Druids since the first days of the Revival. Yet that inspiration must be tempered by the knowledge that a yearning for a richer life can't be satisfied by idolizing somebody else's culture or trying to pretend that you don't belong to the one you actually inhabit. It can only be fulfilled by the hard work of self-knowledge—and that starts from the lived experience of your own place and time.

These issues have special relevance to magic, because a magical tradition is first and foremost a toolkit: a set of methods and tools for making things happen. It's not a cultural fashion statement, a historical reenactment, or a role-playing game, and if it becomes one of these things, it usually stops being effective magic. Judging systems of magic on the basis of their historical authenticity, ironically enough, is also one of the most historically inauthentic things a mage can do, because ancient magical traditions borrowed things from other cultures just as enthusiastically as modern ones do. Since magic is about making things happen, this makes perfect sense, because what matters in a magical system is simply whether or not it works.

All these points apply with particular force to magic as a Druid practice. While Celtic traditions and the legacy of the old Druids inspire modern Druids, the core concerns of Druidry have always centered on the present and the future, not the past. What makes Druid magic relevant today is not whether it comes from an ancient or modern source, but whether it can help restore harmony between humanity and nature. If a Druid magical system can do this, that's all the authenticity it needs.

How to Use This Book

The Druid Magic Handbook has been written as a complete training manual of ritual magic in the modern Druid tradition. Like my earlier book *The Druidry Handbook,* it draws principally on the teachings of the Ancient Order of Druids in America (AODA; *www.aoda.org*), the order I serve as Grand Archdruid. The core practices and traditions of AODA's Druidry are covered in that previous book, including the symbolism and philosophy that underlies the magical system presented here, but everything you need to work this system of Druid magic can be found between the covers of this book.

Still, magic is only one part of the broader Druid tradition, and it works best when practiced together with Druid nature spirituality. Membership in AODA or study of *The Druidry Handbook* open doors to the wider world of Druidry, but these are by no means the only options. The magic taught here also combines well with the study programs of other traditional Druid orders such as the Order of Bards Ovates and Druids (OBOD; *www.druidry.org*) and the Druid Gorsedd of the First Circle (DGOFC; *www.dgofc.org*). Books such as Philip Carr-Gomm's *The Druid Way* are also good sources for such explorations.

Not all of the modern Druid movement shares this much common ground, however. Some recently founded Druid traditions reject the heritage of the Revival, and work with current academic reconstructions of ancient Celtic religion instead. People who prefer this approach to Druidry may find some aspects of the magical work in this book a poor fit with their beliefs. The same will likely be true of followers of other nature-centered religions, such as Wicca, and other traditions of modern magic, such as Hermeticism. I have done my best to make the magic taught in these pages as accessible and inclusive as possible, but no book can be all things to all people.

The eight chapters of this book move through a carefully designed sequence of magical workings, starting from the essential theory and basic practices of Druid magic and proceeding from there through a sequence of progressively more demanding magical workings. If you want to skip around while reading, by all means do that, but if you choose to take up the course of study this book provides, it's important to start at the beginning and work your way through the book a chapter at a time. All the workings in the later chapters are assembled from concepts, rituals, and practices taught early on, and some of the advanced rituals will not work at all unless you do the preliminary practices first. This will likely be true even if you already know another tradition of magic, because Druid magic starts from different principles than most other magical traditions and gathers power from its own distinctive sources.

Patience is essential to the work presented in this book, then. So is your willingness to invest time in the magical practices and studies in this book. Learning magic takes time and practice, just like learning a musical instrument, a martial art, or anything else worth doing. Plan on setting aside twenty to thirty minutes a day, each and every day, for your magical training, as well as periods of up to an hour for magical workings every week or so. If this is more than you can do, this may not be the right time in your life for you to take up magic, and it makes more sense to accept that and set your sights on something within reach than to go through the motions of magical training without any likelihood of getting results.

The other requirements for Druid magic are straightforward. You will need a place to practice magic, but a spare corner of a bedroom or a backyard will meet that requirement. You will also need a few simple magical tools. A set of Ogham sticks or cards, an altar, four small bowls or cauldrons, eight small stones, a wand, another small cauldron, and a bag that can be hung around your neck form the complete toolkit for this book. All of them can be made or bought inexpensively.

You already have the most important tools of magic—your own body and mind, and the living Earth all around you—and all the other magical tools simply help you learn how to tap into a power that has always been all around you. If you are ready to start learning the ways of that power, this book can be your guide.

PART ONE
The Foundations of Druid Magic

CHAPTER I
The Ways of the Life Force

Max Weber, in his famous 1904 book, *The Protestant Ethic and the Spirit of Capitalism,* gave a startling name to one of the realities of modern life: "the disenchantment of the world." Weber was a sociologist who studied the impact of industrial society on human thought. Before scientific materialism seized the imagination of Western culture, he pointed out, people saw the world around them as a place full of magic, where trees and stones could speak, birds traced out the shape of the future in their flight, and those who knew the secret could sense and shape the flow of enchantment in the world around them. This living, breathing, magical world was one of the first casualties of the Industrial Revolution. As materialist beliefs spread, magic trickled out of the world, transforming it—at least in most people's minds—into a mass of lifeless matter relevant only as a source of raw materials or a place to dump waste.

Like most educated people of his time, Weber did not believe in magic. He meant the word *disenchantment* as a metaphor, and he saw the banishing of magic and meaning from the world as a necessary part of progress and the end of an ancient illusion. Still, he recognized that the psychological and spiritual price of progress weighed heavily on the modern world—heavily enough, perhaps, to outweigh its material benefits. In a disenchanted world, he showed, even the most basic human values lose their anchor, and the only things left are the mechanical values of profit and efficiency, the basis for what passes for rational thought in a modern industrial society.

The irony of the phrase is that Weber spoke more truth than he realized. Neither he nor most of his readers saw disenchantment as anything but a metaphor. Still, those who know the living power of magic know that Weber's phrase points to a crucial reality. Our world is literally disenchanted. It suffers from a shortage of enchantment that cuts people off from magical realities and makes their lives less meaningful and magical than they could be.

Enchantment is the art of awakening spiritual presences in material things. The word literally means "putting a song in something"—en-*chant*-ment—a turn of phrase that reflects the living experience of a world in which every part of the landscape and every turn of the seasonal cycle sings its meaning to the awakened mind. In traditional societies around the world and throughout history, enchantment has had a vital role in bringing people into harmony with their gods, their environment, and their communities. Magic provided the toolkit for creating and maintaining enchantment. Using magic, the priestesses and wizards of the past wove nature and humanity into a single fabric that kept both balanced and whole.

As far as anyone knows, the Industrial Revolution marks the first time in human history that a civilization tried to banish enchantment from the world. When Weber assessed the results of this experiment in 1904, cracks were already showing in the bright facade of progress. Now, more than a century later, the collapse of communities and collective spiritual life across the Western world has been joined by the specter of catastrophic environmental change. Dwindling fossil fuel reserves, massive ecological changes, and wild swings in the world's climate announce the coming of an age of payback in which the survival of industrial civilization itself stands at risk.

A little more than forty years have passed now since the environmental crisis first forced itself onto newspaper headlines around the world. During that time, a great many historians have traced the roots of our civilization's dysfunctional relationship with nature, and an even larger number of activists have proposed solutions. Magic has rarely seen mention in either context. A handful of perceptive writers have followed Weber's lead and traced out the connections between a way of thinking about the Earth that strips it of enchantment and a way of acting toward it that strips it of everything else. In *The Reenchantment of the World,* one of the best books of this kind, Morris Berman comments:

> For more than 99 percent of human history, the world was enchanted and man saw himself as an integral part of it. The complete reversal of this perception in a mere four hundred years or so has destroyed the continuity of the human experience and the integrity of the human psyche. It has very nearly wrecked the planet as well. The only hope, or so it seems to me, lies in a reenchantment of the world. (Berman, 1981, p. 10)

Yet neither Berman nor the handful of other writers who have pursued these themes have considered the possibility that the best way to reenchant the world is to use the same magical methods that enchanted it in the first place.

Berman himself claims that "we cannot go back to alchemy or animism" (ibid.). Behind this argument stands the immense emotional force of the modern faith in progress, with its conviction that "going back" is the one unforgivable sin. Yet if a traveler on unfamiliar roads finds that he has gone down a blind alley, the only option that will get him out of it is to go back the way he came.

From the perspective of Druidry, a return to magic is simple common sense. Modern Druidry itself was born alongside the Industrial Revolution, crafted by a handful of British visionaries in the early eighteenth century, who saw the first stirrings of today's ecological crises and recognized that the gap between humanity and nature opened by industrial society had to be healed if Western civilization were to survive. The founders of the Druid Revival took the radical step of embracing the name and legacy of the ancient Celtic Druids at a time when "going back" in religious matters was as unthinkable as doing the same thing scientifically and technologically is today. They recognized that what matters about ideas is not how new they are, or for that matter how old they are, but whether they reflect truth in a way that meets the needs of humanity and nature in a particular age.

The revival of magic in recent decades thus speaks to one of the most critical needs of our time. While magic cannot solve today's ecological crisis by itself, it offers crucial tools for healing the gap between humanity and nature. To understand how magic can accomplish this, and to begin making sense of magic itself, we need to pay attention to a part of human experience that has dropped entirely out of modern awareness.

The Mind-Body Problem

For the past four hundred years, one of the major intellectual puzzles in the Western world has been what philosophers call "the mind-body problem." Like most of the really tough conundrums of philosophy, the problem can be stated simply enough. In Western cultures, most people experience themselves as two very different things—a material body, on the one hand, and an apparently nonmaterial mind, self, personality, or soul on the other. The problem is how to explain the connection between them.

Theories about the relationship between mind and body nearly all fall into two camps. The first approach, called *dualism,* claims that there are two completely separate realms of existence, one mental, one material, that somehow come into contact inside each human being and nowhere else in the cosmos. The other, called *reductionism,* claims that only one of them is real, and then finds some way to explain away the other.

Arguments over the mind-body problem have swung like a pendulum from dualist to reductionist viewpoints and back again. Nowadays reductionist approaches are in vogue, and most scientists and many laypeople accept the reductionist claim that mind is a side effect of the physical body's nervous system. This latter notion is quite often presented these days as simple common sense. Like most things labeled "common sense," however, it relies on a whole series of assumptions that may not bear close examination.

The pendulum keeps swinging because dualism and reductionism both have serious problems. Entire books have been written about these problems, and since they don't bear directly on the subject of magic, they can be left to students of the history of ideas. What makes the wild swings of this intellectual pendulum relevant here is that they started abruptly with the birth of materialist science in the seventeenth century.

Before then, people understood the relationship between mind and body in a very different way. They experienced themselves as three things, not two. A third factor—the life force—existed between mind and body and linked them together. In the magical traditions of the Renaissance, this force was called "spirit," from the Latin word *spiritus,* "breath." To this older way of thinking, spirit is the source of life, energy, and vitality, enlivening the dense matter of the body and connecting it with the mind. In the Renaissance view, spirit surrounds and penetrates all material things, uniting them and weaving the universe into a whole.

If this description sounds like something from a very famous movie, there's good reason for that. George Lucas borrowed the concept of "the Force," the power used by the Jedi Knights of his *Star Wars* movies, from teachings about the life force in the Japanese martial arts, where it is called *ki* and has exactly the same properties Renaissance mages assigned to spirit.

The Druid name for the life force is *nwyfre* (pronounced "NOO-iv-ruh"). Nearly every other language on Earth has a word for it, too. The only languages that don't are the ones spoken in the industrial nations of the modern West.

The banishing of the life force from the worldview of industrial society is no accident. The founders of modern materialist science fought hard to keep their newborn ideology free of any trace of the life force, and you can still reduce most scientists to spluttering indignation by mentioning it. Anything that strays too close to vitalism, as modern philosophers call the idea of a life force, comes in for unrelenting criticism. A great part of the prejudice against alternative healing arts in the modern Western world comes from the fact that most of them, unlike the current medical mainstream, treat the life force as a reality and use it to heal.

Thus there's a deep irony in the past four centuries of debate over the mind-body problem. The relationship between mind and body poses no problem at all outside the modern industrial worldview, because anywhere people recognize the existence of the life force, its role in connecting mind

Table 1-1   Some Names for the Life Force

Name	Source
animal magnetism	Western occultism
ankh	ancient Egyptian
astral light	Western occultism
ch'i (also spelled qi)	Chinese
ea	Hawai'ian
emi	Yoruba
etheric substance	Western occultism
ki	Japanese
ni	Lakota (Sioux)
nwyfre	Welsh Druidry
n:um (the : is a click)	Kalahari !Kung
önd	Norse
odic force	Western occultism
orenda	Iroquois
orgone	Reichian psychology
ori	Mongolian shamanism
pneuma	Gnosticism
prana	Hindu yoga
ruach	Hebrew
ruh	Sufi mysticism
secret fire	alchemy
spirit (spiritus)	Renaissance magic
vital life force	Rosicrucian
win-yaan	Thai shamanism

and body is obvious. The relationship only became a problem in the Western world when materialist science threw out the connecting link. It's as though the first modern scientists decided that their chests didn't exist, and then spent four centuries arguing about what could possibly connect their heads with their bellies.

What makes this all the more fascinating is that the life force is not just a theory or a belief. It's something we experience in the same way that we experience our minds and bodies. Outside the industrial West, the life force is just as much a part of life as bodies and minds are. In modern Japan, for example, people still talk about the state of their *ki* on an everyday basis. The word for courage in Japanese is *yuki,* literally "active ki"; depression is *fukeiki,* "sluggish ki"; a strong personality is described by the words *kisho ga tsuyoi,* "the quality of his ki is strong"; and illness is *byoki,* "disturbed ki." The same sort of talk was every bit as common in medieval and Renaissance Europe, and it's just as common in most other traditional societies.

This same way of experiencing the world also has intensely practical consequences. Asian martial arts, for example, treat the life force as an essential factor and use special training methods to strengthen and direct it. When a martial artist breaks a pine board with a punch or shatters a stack of bricks with a palm strike, the life force flowing into the striking hand does the job. A way of looking at the world that enables flesh and bone to shatter wood and brick is clearly something more than a primitive superstition.

People who experience the life force as an everyday reality have no special "sixth sense" lacking in those of us who live in industrial societies. We dwell in the same world and have the same potentials for awareness that they do. The difference is that their vision of reality makes room for the life force, and ours does not. Children in traditional societies learn to pay attention to the life force in themselves and the world because the people around them notice it, talk about it, and treat it as a reality. Children in industrial societies learn not to pay attention to it in exactly the same way. Even so, when people in the modern industrial world talk about gut feelings and hunches, or the "vibes" or "feel" of a person or a place, most of the time they are talking about their own perceptions of flow and pattern in the life force.

The life force is close enough to the surface of awareness that various simple exercises can make most people conscious of it in a few minutes. Here is an example. Read through the following paragraph, and then do the exercise before you read any further.

Start by standing comfortably with your feet parallel or a little toed out, your heels a foot or so apart, and your knees slightly bent. Let your hands hang at your sides, and shake them for a full minute, making them as loose and floppy as possible. Then rub them together for another full minute, keeping them relaxed as you rub. Then hold them in front of you, palms facing one another, as if you were holding a basketball in front of your chest. Breathe slowly and deeply, keep your hands and arms relaxed, and concentrate on your palms. After a full minute of this, begin moving your hands toward and away from each other a short distance, no more than an inch. This is the final step. Keep doing it for a little while, and see what you notice.

What did you experience? Most people, when they do the exercise the first time, as they move their hands back and forth, feel a gentle pressure against their palms, as though their hands were magnets repelling each other. The longer the back-and-forth motion continues, the stronger the sensation of pressure becomes, and if you do the same exercise daily for a week or more, the sensation becomes as firm as if you held a physical object between your palms.

What you feel pressing against your hands, according to the magical view of the world, is the field of life force between energy centers in your palms. Shaking, rubbing, and relaxation, the basis of the exercise, release muscular tensions that block the flow of life force through your body, so that the fields around your hands become strong enough that you notice them. Those fields are always there, whether you notice them or not, and so are similar fields that radiate out from other centers in your body, filling a roughly egg-shaped space that extends a few feet out from you in all directions. Every living thing has a similar field, and so do many of the things people in the industrial world consider nonliving.

As the bridge between mind and matter, the life force can be influenced in many ways using mind, matter, or the two in combination. The exercise you just performed uses body movements to shape the flow of nwyfre. This is a traditional and powerful way of working with the life force. Martial arts and Eastern systems of spiritual practice such as yoga and qigong rely on this and also on breathing exercises, another classic method. Other spiritual and magical systems rely on physical substances that concentrate certain qualities in nwyfre, or on a knowledge of the times and places where nwyfre flows most strongly.

Ritual magic approaches the life force from a different way—the way of imagination. This is another aspect of reality that has come in for more than its fair share of neglect by modern thinkers; to call something "imaginary" nowadays, after all, is to say that it's unreal. Yet imagination is a potent reality.

Imagination, in fact, is the human mind's way of experiencing patterns in the life force. When you imagine something, that image takes shape in the life force around you. The more powerfully you imagine it, the more strongly the image shapes the life force. This equation works the other way as well. When an unexpected thought or feeling drifts into your mind, most of the time what has happened is that you picked up a pattern in the life force created by some other mind. The movement of patterns in life force from mind to mind explains most psychic phenomena, as well as less controversial experiences such as the spread of fads and fashions and the behavior of crowds. It also explains the workings of ritual magic.

You can begin to see how this works by repeating the same exercise you just did with a slight difference. When you move your hands to face each other, imagine that an actual ball appears between your palms. See it, but also imagine the feeling of it pressing against your palms, and notice the texture of the ball's surface. Concentrate on the imaginary ball as intensely as you can for a full minute, and then start moving your hands toward and away from each other slightly, as before. Do this now, before you read any further.

What did you experience when you started moving your hands back and forth? Most people find that the sensation of pressure becomes much more intense once mental imagery comes into play. If you do the same exercise daily for a week or more with the mental imagery, and then try just imagining the ball without any of the preliminary movements, you'll find that you can sense the fields of life force as soon as you bring your hands together.

This simple process contains the art of ritual magic in miniature. Visualizing the ball and bringing your hands together is a simple ritual. The more you practice it, the more readily the life force responds to it, and magical results follow.

Magic and Nature

In Welsh Druid tradition, nwyfre—the life force—is one of three basic principles of existence. The other two are *gwyar* (pronounced "GOO-yar"), the principle of flow, and *calas* (pronounced "CAH-luss"), the principle of matter. Lift your hand in front of your face and all three elements are right in front of you. Calas is the physical substance of the hand—the skin, flesh, and bone that make it a material object. Gwyar is the movement and flow of the hand—the motion that brings it in front of your face, to begin with, but also the circulation of blood and lymph, and all the other subtle motions that make it what it is. Nwyfre is the life, vitality, and sensation of the hand—the presence of the life force that makes it a living, active, and sensitive thing rather than a dead object.

According to these same Druid traditions, these three things exist in everything in the world. A stone contains gwyar and nwyfre as well as calas; stone flows very slowly, and its life is hard for human beings to perceive, but both are there. A fall breeze contains calas in the form of molecules of oxygen, nitrogen, and other gases, as well as dust and water vapor; gwyar in the form of the movement that sweeps these molecules along; and nwyfre in the form of a simple life and awareness that old magical textbooks call a *sylph,* or air elemental. These and everything else in the world have a basis in matter, a pattern of flow, and an indwelling life: calas, gwyar, and nwyfre, in the language of Druid magic.

The living Earth herself is no exception to this rule. She includes calas in the form of all the solid, liquid, and gaseous matter drawn together by gravity into this little corner of space; gwyar in the form of all the intricate tapestry of movement in, on, and around the Earth, from the great arc of its orbit around the Sun to the wriggling of the smallest single-celled organism in her oceans and soil; and nwyfre in the form of the common life that Renaissance occultists called *spiritus mundi,* the earth spirit, and many modern ecologists call *Gaia.*

The force that makes magic work, in other words, is just as much a part of nature as matter and motion. This isn't the way most people in the modern world think about magic, of course. Ask most people who have never practiced magic what it is, and the word *supernatural* usually shows up in the answer—meaning, among other things, that magic violates the laws of nature. The magic done by characters in films and fantasy novels does this, and most skeptics have this sort of magic in mind when they reject it as impossible. This just doesn't happen to be the sort of magic that mages—people who do magic—actually practice.

Real magic is natural, not supernatural. It unfolds from the natural force of nwyfre, and its effects follow natural patterns and obey the laws of nature. Thus magic won't make rocks fall upward or apple trees bear tomatoes, it won't make matter or energy appear from nowhere or disappear without a trace, and if you were born with brown hair, magic won't make it blonde; you'll have to use hair dye instead. Magic can start, stop, speed up, or slow down anything in nature—including human nature—within the broad limits nature herself sets on those processes. What nature doesn't do, however, magic won't do either.

Accounts of what mages actually do make this point with a high degree of clarity. One of the very best resources along these lines is Vine Deloria Jr.'s extraordinary 2006 book *The*

World We Used to Live In, a collection of accounts of native medicine people and their powers, ranging from the subtle to the spectacular. Deloria's examples include all the things that mages around the world have always done—healing illnesses, finding hidden objects, communicating with birds and animals, shaping weather, making crops fertile, perceiving things distant in space and time, and causing vivid sensory hallucinations in other people. Each of these things happens in keeping with the ordinary patterns of nature, even when the connection between magical cause and physical effect can't be explained by current scientific theories.

Consider a type of magic that sorcerers and shamans have done for thousands of years: a ritual for rain. Nobody who does this kind of magic claims that a successful ritual makes rain fall miraculously out of a clear blue sky. Instead, the barometric pressure drops, the wind shifts, clouds roll in, and rain starts to fall in the normal way. The result looks just like any ordinary rainstorm. It's the way that rain responds to the ritual that makes it magical.

Thus, what makes magic magical, in other words—and what makes materialist skeptics reject it with such heat—is simply that it challenges modern assumptions about cause and effect. Most scientists believe that material effects must have material causes, and the idea that an intention held in the mind, channeled through nwyfre, can set off effects in nature is unthinkable to them. The fact that this is an everyday experience for mages does nothing to make it more palatable! Still, only the role of nwyfre in bridging the gap between mind and matter goes beyond what current scientific theories can explain. Once the ritual gives the rain a starting push, the rest of the process unfolds like any other storm.

One interesting effect of this principle is that skeptics can always insist that the results of magic might be coincidence. When a shaman works a rain spell, it could be coincidence that a rainstorm rolls in a few hours later. If the same spell works a hundred times in a row, it could still be coincidence. As long as the rain spell gets the results the shaman wants, it hardly matters, and indeed magic could almost be defined as the art of causing coincidences in accordance with intention. Think about how many important things in life are governed by what modern people call "coincidence," and you may begin to grasp the astonishing power magic has to shape the universe of human experience.

Still, recognizing that magic is part of nature and governed by natural limits is a crucial step in using it wisely. Neither magic nor anything else in nature has unlimited power. Magic is not a ticket to godhood or a substitute for the more basic disciplines of spiritual practice. It's simply a useful and powerful craft that, like several other traditional crafts, blends well with Druid spiritual practices and a life in harmony with nature. In a world where enchantment is in short supply, however, the gifts magic can offer are desperately needed.

Magic and Intentionality

These considerations are important because harmony with nature is one of the essential principles of Druid magic. With two other themes, symbolism and intentionality, it forms a triad of principles that underlie everything in this book. Symbolism has a role in magic complex enough that it needs a chapter of its own; it is covered in detail in chapter 2 of this book. Intentionality is simpler, but it has depths that many students of magic miss.

For just over a century and a half, most books on magic in the Western world have talked about intentionality in terms of the development and use of the magical will. This habit goes back to the great nineteenth-century French occultist Eliphas Lévi, whose writings launched the modern revival of magic. Lévi got the idea of the magical will from the German philosopher Arthur Schopenhauer, one of the few thinkers of his time to accept the possibility of magic. Schopenhauer saw the universe as the product of a cosmic will creating representations in the minds of beings. In Lévi's writings, this dance of will and representation became a recipe for magical power that used will and imagination to shape the world.

In Lévi's wake, many students of magic came to see magical training as a matter of building up vast reserves of willpower and using them to force the universe to do their bidding. This was not what Lévi meant, as it happens, but some of the colorful language Lévi used to express his ideas helped foster the idea that magic was basically a way of browbeating the universe into getting what you want, when, where, and how you want it. This sort of thinking became popular in magical circles because it resonated with popular ideologies of the time that celebrated humanity's supposed "conquest" of nature.

Like the attitude that sees nature as something to conquer, however, this approach to magic has serious problems. Because it ignores the momentum and flow of natural patterns, it's clumsy and wasteful of energy. It's much like trying to cross a lake on a rowboat without paying attention to the winds and currents. If you ignore these, you can put plenty of effort into rowing and make very little headway, or even end up further away from your goal than you started.

Many people who reject this approach go to the opposite extreme and embrace a passive approach to the spiritual world. Most mainstream religions in the Western world, for example, insist that magic is wrong and people ought instead to pray to a god and then prayerfully accept whatever the god decides to send them. This latter claim, to return to our boating metaphor, is like trying to cross a lake on a rowboat by throwing the oars overboard and trusting the winds and currents to get you to the other side. If you do that, you may cross the lake or you may not, and an attitude of prayerful acceptance of whatever happens is probably a good idea!

These two ideas form what Druid philosophy calls a "binary." A binary is a pair of ideas, factors, or forces in opposition to each other. Binaries exert a curious magnetism on the human mind. Once we get caught up in thoughts of yes or no, right or wrong, love or hate, truth or falsehood, or any other binary, it can be hard to realize that the two poles of the binary don't contain all of reality. The two attitudes just outlined make an excellent example of a binary, because both are extreme positions masquerading as the only two options.

Druid philosophy offers a useful tactic in situations of this kind. When you encounter a binary, you simply look for a third factor that is not simply a midpoint between the two poles. Find the third factor and you convert the binary into a *ternary,* a balanced threefold relationship that allows freedom and flexibility.

In this case, the third factor that resolves the binary into a ternary is knowledge. If you learn how to read the winds and currents, you can work with them rather than against them. You can choose a time when the wind is blowing in the direction you want to go and row yourself into a current that moves in the same direction. As your knowledge develops, you can even turn one oar into a mast, use the other one as a rudder, find a piece of cloth to serve as a sail, and go skimming across the lake with one hand on the tiller and a fair wind doing all the work.

This last approach is the way of Druid magic. Because Druid mages know that they are part of nature, participating in the great dance of life, they pay attention to the movements of that dance and use those movements to get where they want to go. Rather than trying to force the world to do what they want, or sitting around waiting for someone else to do it for them, they learn to make contact with the currents of nwyfre that flow through the world, catch these in the "sails" of their magic, and ride them to their destination.

This is how the magical will actually works. It has nothing in common with Victorian notions of willpower but the word *will*. Think of someone exerting willpower, and what comes to mind? Someone with clenched jaw, white knuckles, narrowed eyes, and rigid muscles? All these signs of conflict betray weakness, not strength. Real will is effortless. It corresponds, not to struggle and strain, but to what philosophers call "intentionality," the orientation of the mind that locates meaning in objects of experience.

An old Hindu metaphor helps show how this works. Imagine that you are walking in the forest and see what looks like a poisonous snake coiled up beside the trail. Heart pounding and muscles ready to jump, you make a wide circle around it, and only then see that it is actually a coil of rope. The object was the same all along, but your mind gave it two radically different intentionalities. When the intentionality changed, everything about your experience changed except the thing you were experiencing.

You may not be able choose whether the coiled thing beside the trail is a snake or a rope. If you face a window and look toward it, however, you can look *through* the window at the scenery outside, or you can look *at* the window and examine the glass, frame, and so on. If you look at the scenery it can be very hard to notice the window glass, and if you look at the glass it can be just as hard to notice the scenery. Is the glass a way of seeing outside or something to look at in its own right? It can be either one, and the difference is intentionality.

Many things in life can be shaped even more powerfully by your choice of intentionality. If you face a challenge with confidence, for example, your chances of success are much better than if you face the same challenge full of doubts and worries. Intentionality is the reason why. What the confident person sees as potential opportunities, the worried person sees as potential obstacles, and they are both right, because whether something is an opportunity or an obstacle usually depends on how you choose to approach it.

Magical philosophy goes one step further than this, because *nwyfre follows intentionality*. When your mind locates meaning in something, nwyfre picks up and amplifies that meaning. The more intense the experience of meaning, the stronger the flow of nwyfre it sets in motion, and the more likely it is to shape other people's experiences as well as yours.

The difference between intentionality and ordinary ideas of willpower explains many of the failures that bedevil beginners. When you try to use magic to will the world into obedience, you set up an intentionality of conflict between yourself and the world. Nwyfre follows that intentionality, and you find yourself embroiled in conflict with everything around you. The harder you try to make the world obey, the more it fights back, because all your efforts reinforce the intentionality and amplify the conflict. Change your intentionality to one of moving in harmony with the world, and the conflict disappears.

The same effect shapes magic's practical applications. Many beginners, for example, try to use magic to achieve financial prosperity, and it's common for their efforts to backfire and leave them poorer than they started. Why? In many cases, their magic focuses on wanting what they don't have. This sets up an intentionality of wanting and not having, and so they end up wanting money and not having it. As with so many things in life, the more energy they put into chasing something, the faster it runs away.

If you want to use magic to become prosperous, your intentionality has to focus on *being* prosperous, not on *wanting* to be prosperous. One effective approach starts with noticing the prosperity already in your life—if you have a roof over your head, three meals a day, and the leisure to read this book, after all, you have more prosperity than half the people on this planet—and letting the change in focus from wanting to having gently redefine your intentionality toward wealth. Another useful strategy focuses on seeing opportunities for abundance around you. This redefines your surroundings as a source of opportunity, and as nwyfre follows intentionality and shapes experience, opportunities appear.

Magic and Ethics

Intentionality also underlies the ethics of magic. This is controversial territory, because there is no consensus in the occult community about what magical ethics should be, or even whether they exist at all. Some traditions and teachers claim that using magic for anything but pure spiritual advancement is a fatal fall from grace, while others insist that the sole point of magic is fulfilling all one's most selfish desires. From a Druid perspective, this is simply another binary, and practical ethics provide the third factor that resolves it into a ternary.

The phrase "practical ethics" may seem strange, but this shows just how confused today's culture has become. Ethics have nothing to do with the pie-in-the-sky idealism and obedience training too often marketed under that label. Rather, ethics teach practical rules of behavior that explain what works and what doesn't. It's not idealism to point out that if a stove burner is hot enough to cook your dinner, it's hot enough to burn your hand, and there's no freedom to be gained by breaking the rules of sanitation. Ethics work in exactly the same way.

This is especially true of magical ethics. Consider a curse meant to bring misfortune on someone. This sort of magic has a long and ugly history behind it, and it works by setting up an intentionality that turns everything in the target's environment into a source of harm. Done with skill and intensity, it can have highly unpleasant results. The risks are just as unpleasant, however, because magic is like raspberry jam; you can't spread it on anything without getting some on yourself. Thus it's proverbial that people who make a habit of destructive magic end up poor, despised, and marginal, because their workings have predictable effects on their own lives.

This happens because intentionality doesn't just affect the target of a magical working. It defines a whole system that includes the mage, the target, and the whole environment. In a magical curse, the intentionality defines the target as a person who suffers misfortune, but it also defines the environment as a source of misfortune, and the mage as a person who causes misfortune. As a result, the mage becomes more likely to cause misfortune even when he doesn't want to, and the environment becomes more likely to be a source of misfortune to the caster as well as the target. If the mage keeps doing such workings, the object may be different each time, but subject and environment stay the same, and eventually the mage starts having trouble causing anything but misfortune, even in her own life, or experiencing her environment as anything but a source of misfortune.

The same process shapes the results you will get from less obviously corrupt forms of magic. Prosperity magic of the sort mentioned in the previous section makes another good example, because many magical novices think of these workings as a way of getting an unearned financial windfall of some kind. The problem with trying to get something for nothing, in a world of limited resources, is that for somebody to get money and not earn it, somebody else must earn the money and not get it. This intentionality defines a whole system, and the keynote of that system is economic unfairness. People who do magic of this kind thus routinely end up on the receiving end of various kinds of economic unfairness, and quite often lose more than the windfall they hoped to gain.

Of course intentionality works the other way just as effectively. This is one reason that so many traditional occult schools encourage students to study and practice some form of healing. The intentionality of healing, like that of cursing or getting something for nothing, defines a whole system, but it defines the healers as people who bring healing rather than misfortune or unfairness, and it defines their environment as a resource for healing. This helps bring healing to themselves as well as to others.

The moral to this story, so to speak, is that the much-maligned Golden Rule—Do to others what you would want them to do to you—makes a useful touchstone for the ethics of your magical work. If you object to having a particular kind of magical working aimed at you, it's rarely if ever appropriate to aim the same sort of magic at anybody else.

If, as many Druids believe, the principles of magic are ultimately the same as the laws of ecology, one of the lessons of today's environmental crisis also has a good deal of relevance here. You can only dump so much pollution into the biosphere before it shows up in the food you eat, the water you drink, and the air you breathe. From this perspective, unethical magic is simply one more kind of pollution, and the things that usually motivate it—ignorance, arrogance, and shortsighted greed—are the same factors pushing our industrial civilization into a bruising collision with ecological reality today.

Solar and Telluric Currents

As the link between mind and matter and the power behind the magical uses of intentionality, nwyfre stands at the heart of Druid magic. Understand the ways of nwyfre and you know all you need to know about the magical arts. This is less easy than it sounds, however. Nwyfre fills the whole universe, and every mental process and material object in the universe affects it in one way or another. To know its ways completely would therefore take a working knowledge of everything in the cosmos.

Fortunately some of the things that influence nwyfre have much more potent effects than others. The most powerful, for our purposes, are the two primary sources of nwyfre in the little corner of the universe where human beings live. One of these is the Sun, and the other is the heart of the Earth. From these spring the two primary currents of nwyfre used by Druid magic: the solar and telluric currents.

The solar current descends to the Earth's upper atmosphere from the Sun and cascades from there down to the surface. It waxes and wanes according to the position of the Sun in the sky, reaching maximum strength at dawn and noon, but it is present even at midnight; it flows wherever light from the sky can reach, and even penetrates a short distance down into the soil. The other planets of the solar system reflect the solar current to Earth just as they reflect the Sun's light, and their cycles shape the flow of the solar current in ways that can be tracked by astrology and other magical traditions of time. The solar current's traditional symbols in myth and legend are birds such as the eagle, the hawk, and the heron. Magical writings sometimes call it *aud* or *od,* and in alchemy it is the Sun. Its primary symbol in Druid lore is the circle, representing the Sun's orb. It is symbolically masculine, and one of its names is the *current of knowledge.*

The telluric current takes its name from Tellus, an old name for the Earth. It rises up from the heart of the Earth through the crust to the surface, and takes its form and character from the landscape the way the solar current takes its character from the turning planets. Underground water affects it powerfully, and springs and wells where water comes to the surface blaze with it. The serpent and the dragon are the most common symbols of the telluric current in myth and legend. Its names in occult lore include *the secret fire, the dragon current,* and *aub* or *ob,* and in alchemy it is Mercury. Its primary symbol in Druid lore is the triangle, representing its fiery and transforming nature. It is symbolically feminine, and one of its names is the *current of power.*

Most systems of ritual magic in the modern West rely on the solar current exclusively. In writings from these traditions you'll hear plenty of talk about heavens and higher levels of being. Learning magic in these systems takes the form of ascent from lower to higher levels, and the major rituals call down the powers of the planets and stars, or draw down deities into earthly manifestation. All these higher levels and powers, to the Druid way of thinking, are ways of talking about different aspects of the solar current.

A much smaller number of magical traditions in the Western world work exclusively with the telluric current instead. In systems of this sort you'll hear talk about underworlds and deeper levels of existence. Learning magic in these systems takes the form of descent or deepening, and the major rituals bring up energies from within the Earth or call up spirits from the depths. All these underworlds and their powers, to the Druid way of thinking, are ways of talking about different aspects of the telluric current.

Traditions that work with the telluric current have a dubious reputation in modern occult circles, and in a very few cases this reputation has been well earned. Workings from certain medieval handbooks of magic use ritual to summon unbalanced, destructive telluric entities from deep within the Earth, so that the mage can browbeat them with symbols of the solar current, bribe them with sacrifices, and force them to obey his will. This approach is as dangerous as it sounds, and tends to be self-defeating as well, since the entities in question usually do whatever they can to turn the tables on their would-be controller. Some of the imagery in these systems draws on popular religious ideas about devils, and this has encouraged some people—even in the occult community—to think of all telluric magic as devil worship.

This is untrue, and indeed unfair. Most of the occult systems that focus on the telluric current bless and heal as effectively and as often as any system of solar magic, and have nothing to do with Satan or any other figure out of Christian mythology. For that matter, there are unbalanced and destructive magical systems that rely solely on the solar current.

It's quite true that the telluric current expresses itself in the individual through the lower aspects of human nature—the forces of life, love, passion, and power that root in the body—but it's only from the biased viewpoint of an extreme solar perspective that *lower* means *worse*. These aspects of the self are lower in the same way that a foundation is lower than the building it supports. They evolved long ages ago and function without conscious attention, and they also work through centers of nwyfre in the belly, hips, and feet, the lower half of the physical body. The womb center, in the belly about one inch below the level of the navel, is the primary focus of the telluric current in the body.

The solar current, by contrast, expresses itself through what are often called the higher aspects of human nature—our capacities for reason, imagination, abstract knowledge, and impersonal emotion. These aspects of the self are higher than the manifestations of the telluric current in the most straightforward physical sense, since they function through centers of nwyfre in the chest, shoulders, and hands. They also evolved more recently and thus require more conscious attention and development than the body and its passions do.

For most of Western history, spiritual as well as magical traditions have embraced one or the other of these currents, and rather too often, they have rejected the other one. The result of this binary has been a great deal of spiritual and psychological imbalance. Taken to extremes, an obsession with the solar current turns spirituality into an arid pursuit of abstract perfection that abandons the body and its potentials for power and delight. Taken to extremes, an obsession with the telluric current turns spirituality into a quest for raw physical sensation that abandons the mind and its potentials for wisdom and insight.

From a Druid perspective, at least, neither of these extremes is very useful. Far more effective as a starting point for magic is the recognition that both poles of the binary are equally necessary and equally holy. From this comes the realization that the interactions between the currents offer many more possibilities for creative action than either current does on its own.

The two currents can interact in several different ways. On the simplest level, they can balance one another like the two halves of the famous *t'ai-chi* (yin-yang) symbol of Taoism (presented as Figure 1-1). At the point of balance between them, possibilities of freedom and effective action exist that cannot be reached from either one of the currents on their own.

The two currents can also set secondary currents of energy in motion. In the symbolic language of alchemy, heaven and earth give birth to a red king and a white queen. These two currents, the red and white dragons of Celtic legend, reflect the energies of the solar and telluric currents in

Figure 1-1   The T'ai-Chi Symbol

the natural world. They play an important role in sexual polarity, and they also have a place in Druid magical work.

The third relationship between the solar and telluric currents, however, yields the deepest and most powerful results. The two currents can fuse, and this fusion gives rise to a third current: the central secret of Druid magic.

The Quest for the Grail

This third current has many names, but the name we'll use here is the *lunar current*. Unlike the solar and telluric currents, the lunar current does not exist naturally in the individual or the world. It must be made by the balanced fusion of the solar and telluric currents. The art of accomplishing this fusion stands at the heart of Druid magic.

The lunar current is called *aur* and *or* in occult writings. Its primary symbol in magical lore is the crescent Moon, and its mythic symbols include the egg, the jewel, the sacred cup, and the child. It mediates between solar and telluric currents in the same way that the Moon mediates between Sun and Earth. It functions on a higher level than the solar current, since it is still evolving in human beings and must be created consciously, and since its energy centers are located in the head, above the centers of the solar and telluric current. Its primary focus in the body is the pineal center in the middle of the head, behind the base of the nose.

While the telluric current works through the body and its passions, and the solar current acts through the mind and its perceptions, the lunar current expresses itself through the soul and its powers. When the lunar current awakens in an individual, it awakens the inner senses and unfolds into enlightenment. When it awakens in the land, it brings healing, fertility, and plenty.

These three currents play an important if rarely recognized role in one of the world's most magical legends, the strange medieval tale about a maimed king, a land under a curse, and a mysterious cup called the Grail. Like Max Weber's account of the effects of industrial society on the human spirit, the Grail legend is a story of disenchantment. The Grail was a wondrous cup with the power to bring fertility and plenty to the land, but because of an ancient crime—different versions of the Grail legend disagreed about what the crime had been—its guardian, the maimed Fisher King, could no longer use its power, and his kingdom became the desolate Waste Land. Only if a questing knight reached the Grail Castle, beheld the Grail, and asked the right question could the magic of the Grail be restored and the Waste Land flourish anew.

While the legend of the Grail is written in the language of medieval romance and draws on the older and even more challenging language of ancient myth, it tells the same story that Weber put in the more precise but less appealing language of sociology. The original Grail legends first emerged at the same time as the intellectual currents that, centuries later, drove the birth of industrial society and its materialist worldview. When Weber wrote his book, industrial society seemed to have overcome all opposition, yet he and many other people recognized the appalling human cost of that triumph, and the Grail legend itself—revived by nineteenth-century poets and artists as part of their own rebellion against industrial society—had become one of the major cultural icons of the age, a symbol that summed up for many people everything that had been lost in the disenchantment of the world.

The Grail legend has even more relevance today, at a time when environmental crisis and industrialism run amok promise to turn huge swaths of the living Earth into a Waste Land more desolate than anything the storytellers of the Middle Ages could have imagined. Questing, knightly courage, and the art of asking the right questions still has a central role in the task of finding the Grail today, but the magical workings presented in this book can become another way to seek the Grail and reenchant a disenchanted world.

A hint pointing to how this works can be found in the way the traditional symbols of the three currents combine. As mentioned earlier in this chapter, an important magical symbol of the telluric current or secret fire is a triangle with one point upward; a disk like the Sun stands for the solar current, and a crescent Moon for the lunar current. Put the three shapes together, in the order they appear in the human body, and the result is a familiar image (Figure 1-2). How these three forces are used to create the Grail is the subject of this book.

Figure 1-2   The Secret of the Grail

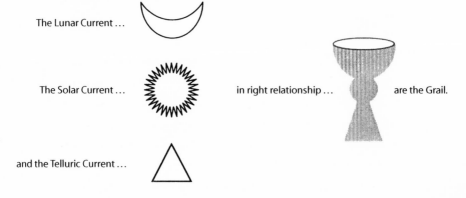

The Lunar Current ...

The Solar Current ...   in right relationship ...   are the Grail.

and the Telluric Current ...

CHAPTER 2
The Alphabet of Magic

Every system of magic has its own ways of working with nwyfre. The art of natural magic, for example, relies on material substances that set up particular patterns in nwyfre. These substances go into amulets, oils, and the like, and they create the desired pattern in nwyfre wherever they are. European peasants thus used to gather the bright yellow flowers of the herb St. John's wort at midsummer and put them over doors and windows to protect against hostile magic, because this herb attracts the solar current and radiates a potent protective quality.

Turn to the art of astrological magic and you encounter a completely different way of working with nwyfre. This branch of magic was invented in ancient Babylon and was passed down through the centuries by Greek, Roman, Arab, and medieval European mages to the Renaissance, when it became the most influential magical system of the age; it is almost extinct now, though a few dedicated scholars still practice it. The astrological mage studies the movements of planets and stars to gauge their relative influences on the solar current. At the moment when some desired quality is at its peak, the mage crafts and consecrates a talisman to catch and store nwyfre full of that quality, and the talisman radiates the pattern placed in it from that moment on.

Either of these two magical systems can be followed as part of a modern Druid path, as indeed can most other magical systems. During the years when magic found its way back into Druidry, however, the most common approach to magic all through the Western world was the art of ritual magic. Developed out of medieval and Renaissance sources by the great French mage Eliphas Lévi in the middle years of the nineteenth century, ritual magic relies on the human imagination to work with nwyfre. As the most widely known and accessible magical system during the revival of Druid magic, ritual magic became the template most twentieth-century Druids used to weave their own magical systems, and it defines the approach used in this book.

In his classic books on magic, Lévi presented a vision of the universe very close to the Druid philosophy outlined in chapter 1. To Lévi, the astral light—his name for the life force—is the "great magical agent," the power that mages wield to accomplish their work. What we call the imagination, Lévi terms the *diaphane,* the subtle body through which the human mind can sense and shape the astral light. Thus dreams and daydreams, stray thoughts, and all the other products of imagination are not simply inside one human brain; some are created by the diaphane of the person who experiences them, others come from outside, but all are projected onto the astral light. When this is done with intention and concentration, it sets up patterns and flows in the astral light, and these accomplish magical effects.

These same ideas form the core of the system of magic presented in this book. What Lévi called the astral light, Druid mages call nwyfre; what he called the diaphane, Welsh Druid tradition calls the *enaid* (pronounced "ENN-eyed"), the body of nwyfre. When a pattern is projected into the enaid with intention and concentration, a Druid mage might say, that pattern takes shape in the nwyfre and sends ripples outward. If that pattern is filled with one or more of the great currents of nwyfre—the solar, telluric, or lunar currents— the ripples that go outward from it have immense power and can shape the world in dramatic ways.

Magical Symbolism

Powerful as it is, this process can be worked very simply. The art of creative visualization, one of the most common practices in today's alternative spirituality scene, is a good example. To practice creative visualization, you simply imagine a situation that you want to bring into your life and make the mental image as rich, detailed, and precise as you can. As you hold the image in your awareness, focus on the idea that by visualizing it, you are bringing that situation into reality. Much more often than not, people who put this method to work find that the desired situation occurs in their lives, often copying their visualization in precise detail.

Many traditional occult schools teach creative visualization to beginning students as a good introduction to the way magic works. In a society that dismisses magic as so much fraud and delusion, the chance to experience it as a living and powerful reality is an important step in magical training, and creative visualization provides that. As a practical technique, though, it suffers from major limitations: most of the time, it takes a great deal of work with the technique to get results from it, and the more emotional investment you have in the situation, the less likely you are to get any results at all.

These limitations unfold from the principle of intentionality. As explained earlier, the intentionality you choose shapes your experience by setting patterns of nwyfre into motion. The more intensely you can concentrate on your intentionality, the stronger the effect will be. It's easier to concentrate on a simple image than a complex set of ideas. In creative visualization, however, a mental picture simple enough to allow intense concentration will usually be too simple to express your intention clearly, and one detailed enough to formulate your intention will usually be too complex to allow intense focus.

Emotional investment amplifies this effect. Most people who try creative visualization to improve their health, say, are motivated by desire and fear—they crave health or fear sickness, or both. Few people have the mental discipline to visualize a scene that touches on desires or fears without stirring up those emotions, and the attention that goes into desiring health or fearing sickness is diverted from the magical work at hand. Worse, since desire and fear both focus on *not* being healthy—the desire fixates on what you would do if your health improves, the fear on what might happen if it does not—you risk setting up an intentionality of wanting to be healthy, rather than one of being healthy, and ending up with the opposite of the effect you want.

The solution to these problems is as old as magic itself. Instead of concentrating on a mental picture of the situation you want to create, you concentrate on an abstract symbol that represents that situation without actually portraying it. You start by stating aloud what you want to bring into being, and then release the words and concentrate entirely on the symbol. Since magical symbols are visually simple, concentrating on them is easier, and since they have no obvious connection to the goal of the work, most novice mages find it much easier to keep unwanted emotions and wandering thoughts from intruding and weakening the process.

Some modern magical systems like to create a unique symbolism for each working. This can work well enough, but most mages find that symbols used repeatedly get stronger results than symbols made up for individual workings. The traditional explanation for this experience is that symbols develop something like momentum in the way they affect nwyfre. The more often a symbol is projected into nwyfre, in other words, the more quickly and powerfully nwyfre responds to it.

This way of thinking about symbols helps avoid two less useful attitudes toward them that are common nowadays. Some people dismiss symbols as a hodgepodge of arbitrary images connected in arbitrary ways. Others go to the opposite extreme and decide that some particular set of symbols express hard and fast truths about the universe—that the element of water is associated with the west and the color blue, let's say, as a matter of objective fact. Neither of these viewpoints fit the way symbols actually function in magic. Traditional symbols and symbolic relationships work well when put to the only test that counts—the test of actual practice—but different systems disagree on how symbols relate to one another. In Chinese Taoist magic, for example, the element of water is associated with the North and the color black, rather than West and blue, but Taoist mages get results just as effectively as Druid mages do.

The key to understanding this is the recognition that all symbols draw their meaning from their context in a whole system. The relationship between west and water, to continue the example, comes out of a particular way of thinking about elements, directions, and much else. To say that the west corresponds to water is to say that within a particular system the west, among the directions, means many of the same things that water means among the elements.

Another way to say the same thing is to suggest that the logic of magical symbolism is closely related to the logic of poetry. In a well-written poem, each turn of phrase and choice of imagery takes its meaning from its context. When the Scottish poet Robert Burns began a poem with the line "My love is like a red, red rose," he didn't mean to suggest that the woman he loved had thorns, or was green from the hairline down, or resembled a rose in any of a hundred other ways. He meant that she was beautiful; more than that, he meant to remind the reader of the way the brilliant red of a rose against the drab greens and browns of the rosebush catches and holds the eye, and used this as an image of the intensity of a lover's gaze focusing on the one he loves. The context of the poem gives the correspondence between woman and rose its meaning.

Some poems use only stock images and phrases that already have a rich context of meaning. Others use images and phrases nobody else has used before. Very often, though, the best poetry combines the familiar and the new in creative ways. Magical symbolism most often works the same way as this third type. There's a good deal of common ground among different systems, but if you compare magical handbooks from the Middle Ages, say, you'll discover that no two of them use exactly the same symbolism. Since no two of the old grimoires work magic in the same way, or for the same purposes, this sort of diversity is unavoidable.

To return to the metaphor of poetry, if *your* love isn't like a red, red rose, but looks like some other flower, then by all means use the words that work for you. As you go through this book, in other words, feel free to experiment with symbols other than the ones I provide. The disadvantage of using a symbolism that does not work for you can easily outweigh the advantage of momentum from using a symbol other people also use. Magic is a creative art, and the personal factor needs to be included in any working.

The Ogham Alphabet

The modern Druid tradition, like most other forms of spirituality, has a wealth of symbols that can be put to work in magic. The three elements and three currents discussed in chapter 1 can be understood and used as symbols, though they also represent real forces that shape the world of our experience. From the beginning of the Druid Revival, though, one particular set of symbols has had a central role in Druid practice.

This is the old Irish alphabet called *Ogham* (pronounced "OH-um"), one of the world's most eccentric writing systems. Ogham letters are called "fews" (*feada* in Irish) and consist of four groups called *aicme,* of one to five tally marks each. There are also five more complex signs, called *forfedha* (literally "extra fews"), used for sounds that weren't part of the original alphabet. The fews are marked along a line—upward from the bottom on a vertical line, and from left to right on a horizontal one, as shown in Figure 2-1. Awkward on paper, Ogham is quick, clean, and very readable if your writing instrument is a knife and your "paper" is a stick, and even better if you're using a chisel on the edges of a standing stone. All over Ireland, Scotland, and the western parts of Britain standing stones carved with Ogham between the third and tenth centuries CE can still be read today.

The ancient Irish and the Picts—the people who lived in Scotland before the Scots got there—used Ogham fews to write names on gravestones and spells on magical objects. By the tenth century, Ogham had been replaced by the

Figure 2-1   Ogham Writing

Both of these inscriptions spell out the word *Ogham*. The arrowhead shape ʌ marks the beginning of the line, which can be the edge of a standing stone or a line drawn on paper, and also shows the direction the Ogham fews are read.

Roman alphabet in general use, but Irish bardic schools kept it alive as a branch of traditional lore for centuries longer, and wove a wealth of symbolism into it. The surviving Irish Ogham treatises connect the fews to trees, colors, and much else, giving them a wealth of possibilities as magical symbols.

As a relic of ancient Celtic tradition the Ogham found its way into modern Druidry from the very beginning. John Toland, who helped launch the Druid Revival in the early eighteenth century, included references to Ogham in his writings, and many other Druid writers in the eighteenth and nineteenth centuries discuss Ogham as a Druid alphabet. By the time Druids began developing the magical side of their tradition in the twentieth century, Ogham provided them with an alphabet of symbols as rich as anything in the Western world's other magical traditions.

The twenty-five Ogham fews, along with some of their meanings, appear on the next few pages. More of their symbolism occurs later in this book, and a more complete list of their meanings can be found in *The Druidry Handbook*. These letters are as important to Druid magic as the letters of English are to reading this book, and the time you spend learning them will not be wasted.

FIRST AICME

Beith (pronounced "BEH"): the letter B
A few of beginnings and purification, symbolized by the birch tree; the potential for renewal and rebirth in every moment

Luis (pronounced "LWEESH"), the letter L
A few of protection, discernment, and inner clarity, symbolized by the rowan or mountain ash tree; the choice between insight and ignorance

Nuin (pronounced "NOO-un"), the letter N
A few of connection, communication, and magic, symbolized by the ash tree; words and meanings weaving the world together

Fearn (pronounced "FAIR-n"), the letter V
A few of oracular guidance, protection, and transitions from realm to realm, symbolized by the alder tree; a bridge over deep waters, the presence of spirit

Saille (pronounced "SAHL-yuh"), the letter S
A few of grace, fluidity, receptivity, and response, symbolized by the willow tree; moving with the flow of events, releasing fixed forms

SECOND AICME

Huath (pronounced "OO-ah"), the letter H
A few of patience, restriction, and desire not yet fulfilled, symbolized by the hawthorn tree; a time of waiting, the presence of danger

Duir (pronounced "DOO-er"), the letter D
A few of power, protection, and change for the better,
symbolized by the oak tree; the opening of a door and
the awakening of strength

Tinne (pronounced "CHIN-yuh"), the letter T
A few of courage, conflict, and opposition, symbolized
by the holly tree; challenges that must be confronted
head on, a time for decisive action

Coll (pronounced "CULL"), the letter C
A few of knowledge, creativity, and inspiration,
symbolized by the hazel bush; a new stage in life,
the awakening of intellect

Quert (pronounced "KWEIRT"), the letter Q
A few of delight, celebration, and choice, symbolized
by the apple tree; rewards of effort, the opportunity to
live more fully

THIRD AICME

Muin (pronounced "MUHN"), the letter M
A few of insight, intoxication, and prophecy, symbolized by the grapevine; unexpected truths, freedom
from the limits of time

Gort (pronounced "GORT"), the letter G
A few of tenacious purpose and indirect progress, symbolized by the ivy bush; a winding but necessary path,
entanglements that cannot be avoided

Ngetal (pronounced "NYEH-tal"), the letter Ng
A few of transformation, healing, and swift movement, symbolized by the reed or broom; the flow of time and the transience of all experienced things

Straif (pronounced "STRAHF"), the letter Z (sometimes ST)
A few of hard necessity and inevitable change, symbolized by the blackthorn tree; the influence of fate, no choice but to go onward

Ruis (pronounced "RWEESH"), the letter R
A few of resolutions, fulfillments, and endings, symbolized by the elder tree; the completion of a path, transition to a new state of being

FOURTH AICME

Ailm (pronounced "AHL-m"), the letter A
A few of vision, understanding, and eminence, symbolized by the fir or pine tree; seeing things in perspective, expanded awareness

Onn (pronounced "UHN"), the letter O
A few of attraction, combination, and possibility, symbolized by the gorse bush; life and energy, a rising curve of growth and potential

Ur (pronounced "OOR"), the letter U
A few of power, creation, death, and rebirth, symbolized by the heather bush; spiritual power and creativity, a door opens in the inner world

Eadha (pronounced "EH-yuh"), the letter E
A few of perseverance, courage, and hard work, symbolized by the aspen tree; courage and tenacity in defense, the quest for inner strength

Ioho (pronounced "EE-yoh"), the letter I
A few of enduring realities and legacies, symbolized by the yew tree; that which abides unchanged, the lessons of experience

THE FORFEDHA

Koad (pronounced "KO-ud"), the letter Ch
A few of central balance and infinite possibility, symbolized by a grove of many trees; the presence of many factors, the possibility of freedom

Oir (pronounced "OR"), the letter Th
A few of fate, sudden change, and the unexpected, symbolized by the spindle tree; the flash of the lightning bolt, change caused by outside factors

Uilleand (pronounced "ULL-enth"), the letter W
A few of secrets hidden and revealed, symbolized by the honeysuckle vine; the influence of the subtle and seemingly insignificant, hidden meanings

Phagos (pronounced "FAH-gus"), the letter F
A few of learning, guidance, and the wisdom of the past, symbolized by the beech tree; the messages of the past as the key to the future

Mór (pronounced "MOHR"), the letter X

A few of beginnings, endings, and the influence of outside forces, symbolized by the sea; the arrival of a new factor, the workings of destiny

Ogham and the Elements

Unless you have studied other magical systems, you may be wondering how these Ogham fews relate to magic at all. The secret lies in the magical practice of *correspondence*. A correspondence is a relationship between two symbols, connecting them with exactly the same sort of poetic logic mentioned earlier in this chapter. These connections give you the raw materials to turn any situation you want to bring about into a symbol you can imagine clearly. They also weave the world together into patterns of shared meaning—the basis for the enchantment of the world.

Each Ogham few has many correspondences, some more useful in magic than others. Among the most useful are the five traditional elements. A quirk of language makes these elements challenging for many modern people to understand, however. Today's science sees elements as basic types of physical matter, each made up of a distinct kind of atom. Hydrogen, for example, is made of atoms with one proton and one electron; helium, of atoms with two protons and two electrons, and so on. This is the only meaning of the word *element* most people know nowadays.

The word originally meant something different, however. Before it was taken over and redefined by chemists in the eighteenth century, elements were understood as conditions of matter, not fixed types, and there were five of them:

earth, water, air, fire, and spirit. Modern scientists heap scorn on this older system, and then go on to describe a universe made of solids, liquids, gases, energy, and the background fabric of spacetime itself—exactly the same concept under different names.

Yet the traditional elements are not simply physical states of matter. Like everything in the old enchanted world, they had connections linking them to everything else in the universe of human experience. Each of the elements corresponds to a season, a direction, a time of day, an emotional state, and much more. Even today, we describe someone prone to anger as hot tempered, someone whose thoughts drift loose from reality as an airhead, and so on. All these metaphors point to symbolic connections that magic can use.

Table 2-1 The Five Elements

Element	Air	Fire	Water	Earth	Spirit
Direction	East	South	West	North	Center
Color	Yellow	Red	Blue	Green	White
Time of Day	Dawn	Noon	Dusk	Midnight	Now
Animal	Hawk	Stag	Salmon	Bear	Human
Symbol		△	▽		○

The five elements have these basic qualities:

Air opens, expands, clarifies, and connects. The old elemental lore calls it warm and moist—that is, it radiates energy and responds to its surroundings. It corresponds to the east, dawn, spring among the seasons, and the intellect in the self.

Fire illuminates, challenges, transforms, and destroys. Elemental lore calls it warm and dry—that is, it radiates energy and does not respond to its surroundings. It corresponds to the south, noon, summer among the seasons, and the will in the self.

Water receives, resolves, unites, and dissolves. The old elemental lore calls it cold and moist—that is, it absorbs energy and responds to its surroundings. It corresponds to the west, dusk, autumn among the seasons, and the emotions in the self.

Earth closes, limits, establishes, and manifests. The old elemental lore calls it cold and dry—that is, it absorbs energy and does not respond to its surroundings. It corresponds to the north, midnight, winter among the seasons, and the senses in the self.

Spirit originates, witnesses, and reabsorbs all the other elements. The old elemental lore gives it no qualities of its own, because all qualities unfold from it. It corresponds to the center, the present moment, and pure awareness in the self.

In certain Druid traditions—including that of AODA, the source of the magical system taught in this book—the element of spirit is further divided into three elements: Spirit Above, Spirit Below, and Spirit Within, corresponding to nwyfre, gwyar, and calas. This fits an old symbolism that assigns the number 3 to spirit, the number 4 to matter, and the number 7 to the universe, which is made of both. Several important parts of the ritual work in this book use this system of seven elements.

The symbolism of the Ogham uses the more basic set of five elements. It adds another level of complexity, however, because each few represents a combination of two elements, not a single element on its own. Each of the five elements can be divided into five subelements; air, for example, has a spiritual side, a fiery side, an airy side, a watery side, and an earthy side, and so on for all the other elements.

Table 2-2 shows how this works. Each aicme of five fews represents one of the five elements, and each few in the aicme is a subelement of that element. Thus Beith is the spiritual side of the element of air, Luis the fiery side of air, Nuin its airy side, Fearn its watery side, and so on through the list of fews to Mór, the earthy side of spirit. In this way the Ogham alphabet gives the Druid mage access to a precise set of symbols for elemental forces.

Table 2-2   Ogham and the Elements

Beith: Spirit of Air	Muin: Spirit of Water
Luis: Fire of Air	Gort: Fire of Water
Nuin: Air of Air	Ngetal: Air of Water
Fearn: Water of Air	Straif: Water of Water
Saille: Earth of Air	Ruis: Earth of Water
Huath: Spirit of Fire	Ailm: Spirit of Earth
Duir: Fire of Fire	Onn: Fire of Earth
Tinne: Air of Fire	Ur: Air of Earth
Coll: Water of Fire	Eadha: Water of Earth
Quert: Earth of Fire	Ioho: Earth of Earth
Koad: Spirit of Spirit	
Oir: Fire of Spirit	
Uilleand: Air of Spirit	
Phagos: Water of Spirit	
Mór: Earth of Spirit	

It's important to take the time to think through these correspondences, and see how each few combines the elemental forces that go into it. Later on, we'll discuss other practices—meditation and scrying—that will help you explore these correspondences and others in more depth, in preparation for using them in magic. The simple process of thinking about them and trying to see how the meaning of the few unfolds from the combination of the elements, however, offers a good starting place for this work.

Ogham and the Two Currents

The elements are only part of the full symbolism of the Ogham alphabet, however. Another part can best be approached through the work of two of the twentieth century's most influential writers on Ogham. The first of them, Robert Graves, was neither a Druid nor an occultist. He was a poet and writer, one of the "War Poets" whose work voiced the bitterness of the generation that survived the trenches of the First World War, and a passionate if somewhat eccentric student of mythology.

In 1944, as Graves waited out the Second World War in a small village in Devonshire and worked on a novel about the Argonauts, he found his mind haunted by the Ogham and its relationship to mythology. Setting the novel aside, he launched into a book on Ogham and myth called *The Roebuck in the Thicket,* finishing a 70,000-word manuscript on the subject in three weeks. After the war ended, he returned to his home in Majorca and turned the manuscript into the book that introduced Ogham to the Neopagan scene: *The White Goddess.*

Graves and his mythic interpretation of Ogham have come in for more than their share of controversy in recent years. Some people in the Pagan community accepted Graves' theories as historical fact. Others reacted against this by dismissing Graves as a purveyor of hokum. Both missed the point that Graves was a poet, not a historian, and *The White Goddess* is an intensely personal poetic vision of mythology, not a history textbook.

As a brilliantly constructed work of poetic symbolism and myth, *The White Goddess* makes very poor history but excellent poetry—and as suggested earlier in this chapter, what makes good poetry also makes good magic. This insight guided the second of our two Ogham authors, Colin Murray, in making sense of Ogham as a Druid magical alphabet for today.

Murray, an architect and antiquarian with a passion for Celtic studies, was a major presence in the British Druid scene in the second half of the twentieth century. The Druid order he founded, the Golden Section Order (GSO), always remained small but had a massive influence on other Druid groups all over the world. Among his other achievements, he created the first Ogham divination system in modern times, and nearly all books on Ogham printed since the 1970s borrow from his work.

One of the chief things Murray drew from Graves was a way of arranging the twenty primary Ogham letters in a *dolmen arch,* as shown in Figure 2-2.

Graves created this diagram to explain one of the features of his Ogham system, a lunar calendar with thirteen months named after thirteen of the Ogham consonants. The months begin at the winter solstice with the letter *Beith,* marked here as *B,* on the bottom of the left-hand pillar, and rise up to *Saille,* marked as *S,* on the lintel stone above. *Straif,* shown as *Z,* shares Saille's month, which is why it appears on the end of the lintel stone next to *S.* The months then proceed from left to right from Saille through Huath, Duir, and Tinne to Coll and Quert, which share a month. The calendar turns down the right-hand pillar at C, and descends through Muin,

Figure 2-2   The Dolmen Arch

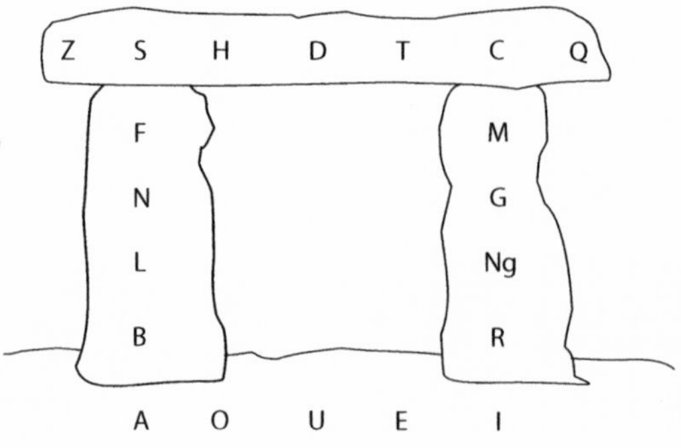

Gort, and Ngetal to Ruis at the bottom. The five vowels *Ailm, Onn, Ur, Eadha,* and *Ioho* mark the ground below the arch, because they represent specific days—the solstices and equinoxes—rather than months.

Murray noted that the figure puts Duir the oak-few at the top center and Ur the heather-few at the bottom center. The oak, because it attracts lightning and is sacred to sky gods in many cultures, has long been a symbol of the power of the heavens. The heather, because of its magical powers and its place as an ingredient in heather ale, a magnificently intoxicating beverage, has long been a symbol of the power of the Earth. The meanings of the two Ogham letters link them to two forms of an ancient magical symbol—the pentagram (Figure 2-3).

A *pentagram* is a star made of five equal lines meeting at five equal angles. Since the time of Pythagoras, who brought sacred geometry to the Western world in the sixth century BCE, it has been one of the core symbols of Western magic and spirituality. It has had many meanings down through the years. Modern Pagans who think of it as a purely Pagan symbol, for instance, may be startled to find it in the medieval poem *Sir Gawain and the Green Knight* as an emblem of Christian virtues!

Figure 2-3 The Pentagram

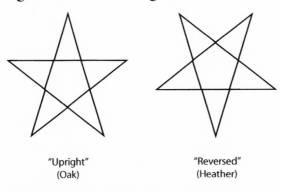

"Upright"
(Oak)

"Reversed"
(Heather)

The Alphabet of Magic

In modern magical practice, it stands for the power of the element of spirit in relation to the four material elements. A moral dimension goes along with this interpretation in most magical writings: a pentagram with a single point upward is considered "upright" and stands for spirit ruling over the four elements, while a pentagram with a single point downward is called "reversed" and stands for spirit submerged beneath the four elements. The upright pentagram thus serves as a symbol of good, and the reversed pentagram an emblem of evil.

All this, however, depends on the assumption that spirit is always and only above—in the terms introduced in chapter 2, that the solar current is good and the telluric current is evil. That assumption is very common in modern occultism, but it's no less wrong for being popular. Recognize the telluric current as a power just as holy and necessary as the solar current, and the relationship between the pentagrams takes on a new and more balanced meaning.

Murray applied this insight to Graves' Ogham diagram and turned it into a potent tool for Druid magic. Map the pentagrams onto the dolmen arch, and the Ogham fews give new names to each form. The upright or solar pentagram touches Duir with its uppermost point, so in Druid practice this form is called the "oak pentagram" (Figure 2-4). The

Figure 2-4 The Oak Pentagram

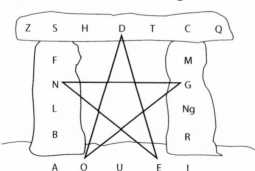

reversed or telluric pentagram touches Ur with its lower-most point and is therefore called the "heather pentagram" (Figure 2-5). As symbols of the solar and telluric currents respectively, the oak and heather pentagrams allow you to work with the two currents in ritual.

Ogham and the Wheel of the Year

Graves' thirteen-month Ogham calendar has seen some use in modern Druidry, but long before Graves came along, Druidry had its own sacred calendar. From the beginnings of the Druid Revival, the tradition of watching the summer solstice at Stonehenge provided the anchor point for that calendar, and by the late eighteenth century the winter solstice and the equinoxes had been added to create a fourfold cere-monial calendar that followed the dance of Sun and Earth.

This calendar remained standard in the Druid community until the early 1950s, when Ross Nichols and his fellow Druid Gerald Gardner, the founder of modern Wicca, took it a step further. Gardner found references in Irish and Scottish sources to an old sacred calendar with four festivals—*Samhuinn, Imbolc, Belteinne,* and *Lughnasadh,* to give them their usual Druid names—midway between the solstices and equi-noxes, and he used this fourfold calendar in the first version

Figure 2-5 The Heather Pentagram

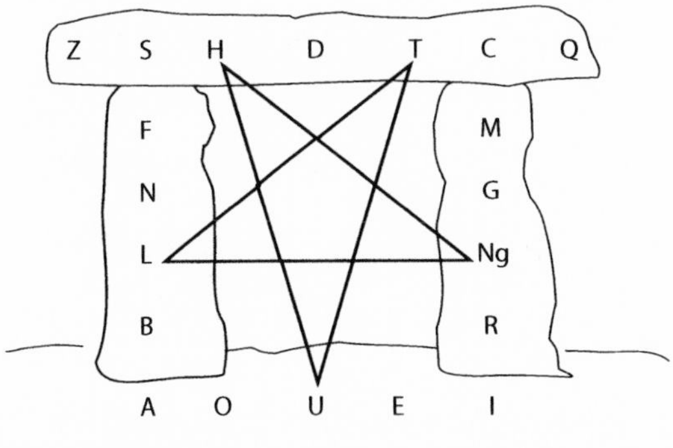

of his newly created nature religion, then called "Wica." Both men were members of the Druid Circle of the Universal Bond, one of the largest Druid orders of the time, and they knew the standard Druid calendar well. Their inspiration was to fuse the two into an eightfold calendar (Figure 2-6). According to a tradition current in English Druid circles today, the inspiration for the eightfold wheel of the year happened in a London pub after several pints of ale; if this is true, it was not the only important event in Druid history to take place in a pub!

The new calendar caught on rapidly, and today most Pagans throughout the Western world use the eightfold wheel of the year. Many of them believe that this calendar dates back to ancient times. In point of fact, no trace of a ritual calendar based on these eight festivals, and only these festivals, appears anywhere before Gardner and Murray publicized their version, and the eightfold calendar has accordingly come in for the same sort of criticism as Graves' Ogham system. Once again, though, such criticism misses the point. A ritual calendar, like a magical alphabet, has value because it works, not because it has (or lacks) a particular historical pedigree.

Nichols and Gardner were both expert occultists, and they created something much more potent than a simple calendar. Understood in depth, the wheel of the year models every process in the universe of human experience as a cycle of eight stations (see Table 2-3), driven by two balanced forces moving around a third, central pivot. The eight festivals can be seen as eight archetypal realms of being, like the spheres of the Cabalistic Tree of Life used in the Golden Dawn and many other magical traditions. Connect these Stations with the twenty-five fews of the Ogham alphabet, and the result

Figure 2-6　The Wheel of the Year

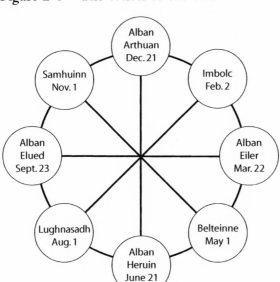

Table 2-3　The Eight Stations

Station	Planet	Element	Colors	Emblem
Samhuinn	Moon	Gwyar	Violet and silver	Cauldron
Alban Arthuan	Sun	Nwyfre	White and gold	Crown
Imbolc	Earth	Calas	Brown and black	Circle of candles
Alban Eiler	Saturn	Earth	Indigo and red	Dragon
Belteinne	Jupiter	Water	Sky blue and orange	Hirlas (mead horn)
Alban Heruin	Mars	Fire	Red and yellow	Three Rays
Lughnasadh	Venus	Air	Gold and green	Fiery wheel
Alban Elued	Mercury	Spirit	Leaf green and blue	Silver branch

is the Wheel of Life, one of the core conceptual tools of Druid magic (Figure 2-7).

Like the Cabalistic Tree of Life, the Wheel of Life defines a set of magical states of consciousness and realms of experience and provides pathways to move from one to another.

Figure 2-7 The Wheel of Life

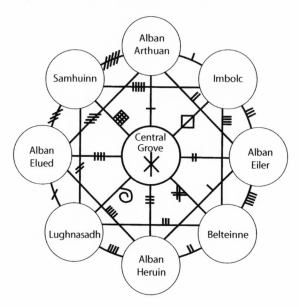

Both the Wheel and the Tree have thirty-three elements: 10 Spheres plus 22 Paths plus a transitional realm called *Daath* or Knowledge make up the Tree of Life; 8 Stations plus 24 Paths plus the Central Grove make up the Wheel of Life. (Figure 2-8 shows how the two diagrams compare.) From a deeper perspective, the two diagrams are alternative ways of looking at the same set of relationships, and meditating on the relationship between them opens the door to many mysteries.

The Tree and the Wheel are not identical in structure or operation, though, and several crucial differences divide them. One is that the Tree is based on a map of space, while the Wheel is a map of time. The spheres of the Tree are assigned to parts of the Earth-centered cosmos of the Middle Ages— the bottom sphere is the Earth, the seven above it are the

Figure 2-8   The Tree of Life and the Wheel of Life

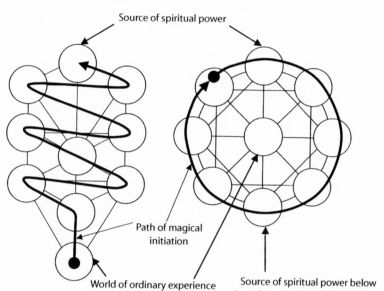

seven planets known before the discovery of the telescope, the ninth is the realm of the stars, and the tenth represents the divine realm beyond the stars.

The Wheel, by contrast, follows the cycle of the seasons. Instead of seeing the great realms of existence as worlds far from our own, it pictures them as phases of time that manifest right here on Earth in cyclic patterns. These same patterns appear in smaller cycles of time—for example, the old Welsh Druid lore divides the day into eight parts, corresponding to the Stations of the Wheel, and the lunar cycle can also be divided into eight parts. All these can be used to time magical workings, and each Station is at its strongest when its daily, monthly, and yearly times occur together. The correspondences among these phases are shown in Table 2-4.

Table 2-4   The Stations in the Day and Lunar Month

Station	Time of Day	Phase of Moon
Samhuinn	Ucher (evening, 9:00–11:59 PM)	Last Crescent
Alban Arthuan	Dewaint (midnight, 12:00–2:59 AM)	New Moon
Imbolc	Pylgeint (first light, 3:00–5:59 AM)	First Crescent
Alban Eiler	Bore (dawn, 6:00–8:59 AM)	First Quarter
Belteinne	Anterth (morning, 9:00–11:59 AM)	Waxing Gibbous
Alban Heruin	Nawn (noon, 12:00–2:59 PM)	Full Moon
Lughnasadh	Echwydd (afternoon, 3:00–5:59 PM)	Waning Gibbous
Alban Elued	Hwyr (dusk, 6:00–8:59 PM)	Last Quarter

Another major difference between the Tree of Life and the Wheel of Life lies in the way the process of magical initiation appears on them. The Tree shows magical initiation as an upward journey from the lowest sphere of ordinary consciousness, called *Malkuth* in the Cabala, to the highest sphere of universal consciousness, called *Kether*. The Wheel, by contrast, shows magical initiation as a continuing cycle around a point of balance—the Central Grove—from which all states of consciousness can be accessed at once.

This echoes some of the core concepts of the Druid tradition. From the standpoint of Druidry, after all, the material world is just as holy as any other, and spiritual practice is not a matter of abandoning one state of being for another, supposedly higher one, but rather of embracing the full potential of what it means to be human and learning to be present in whatever mode of being is most relevant at any given moment. The vision of the process of initiation as a circle also teaches what every magical initiate knows, that the way of initiation has to be walked many times, not just once.

The difference between the two diagrams, finally, has important practical applications in magical work. The Tree of Life orients the mage toward a single source of spiritual power, the universal consciousness of Kether, but the Wheel of Life places the mage in a relationship with two sources, the solar current above and the telluric current below. In one sense, those are represented by two Stations: Alban Heruin, the summer solstice, represents the solar current, while Alban Arthuan, the winter solstice, represents the telluric current. This is a simplified model, though. On another level, the solar and telluric currents manifest through each of the Stations, and what moves the currents from Station to Station is the factor of time.

Imagine for a moment that you are standing in the Central Grove with half the Wheel rising high above you and the other half sinking far below. Above you is Alban Arthuan, as in Figure 2-6, and below you is Alban Heruin. During the season of Alban Arthuan, the six weeks or so following the winter solstice, this is an accurate map of the currents: the solar current flows through the Station of Alban Arthuan, while the telluric current flows through the Station of Alban Heruin.

Six weeks pass, the Wheel of Life turns an eighth of the way around its cycle, and Imbolc arrives. Imbolc is now overhead, Lughnasadh is below, and these two Stations mediate the solar and telluric currents respectively. Six more weeks pass, and Alban Eiler directs the solar current while Alban Elued channels the telluric current. In the course of the year, both currents flow through each of the eight Stations in turn.

This is the magical meaning of the eight festivals of the modern Druid year. Each festival represents the point at which the solar and telluric currents shift to new Stations on the Wheel. The Station occupied by the solar current is the festival being celebrated, while the telluric current flows through the Station at the opposite point of the Wheel.

Celtic folklore hints at this double cycle in stories about another world, the world of the faeries or the dead, where the seasons are exactly opposite to ours. This "other world" lies beneath the surface of the Earth, in the realm of the telluric current, and the cycle of its nwyfre through the eight Stations forms one of the secrets of Druid magic.

The key to this secret lies in the pentagram. You learned earlier in this chapter that the oak and heather pentagrams allow you to summon nwyfre from the solar and telluric currents. This is the most important use of the pentagrams, but it conceals a more complex and flexible use. The upper point of the oak pentagram, and the lower point of the heather pentagram, represent the solar and telluric currents *and whatever Station they occupy at the time the pentagram is drawn*. The other points of both pentagrams, in turn, represent the other Stations of the Wheel, as shown in Figure 2-9.

Figure 2-9   Pentagrams on the Wheel of Life

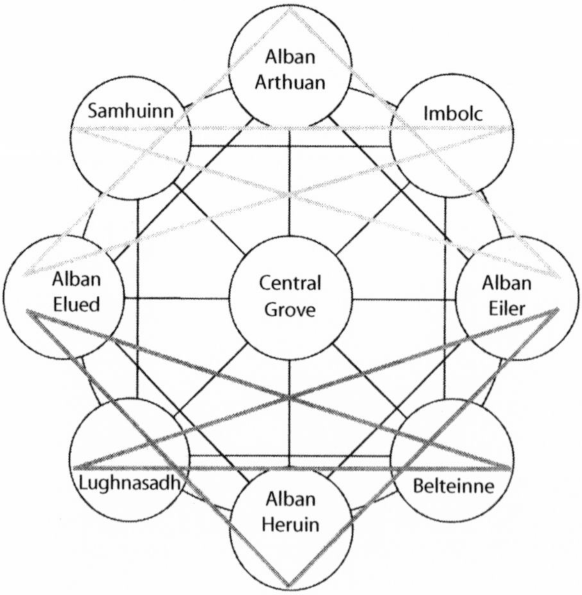

Part One: The Foundations of Druid Magic

The three Stations in the solar realm—represented by the upper half of the wheel—are always summoned and banished with the oak pentagram, and the three in the telluric realm—the lower half of the wheel—are summoned and banished with the heather pentagram. The two Stations that stand on the boundary between the solar and telluric realms can be summoned or banished with either one. It's best, however, to use the oak pentagram for the Station on the right-hand side, because this one is rising into the solar realm, and to use the heather pentagram for the Station on the left-hand side, because this one is setting into the telluric realm.

The point that has to be grasped in all this is that the point you use for any given Station depends on the season of the year. Six weeks after Alban Arthuan, when Imbolc arrives, the Stations shift to the positions shown in Figure 2-10. Six weeks or so later, when Alban Eiler arrives, they shift again,

Figure 2-10 The Rotation of the Stations

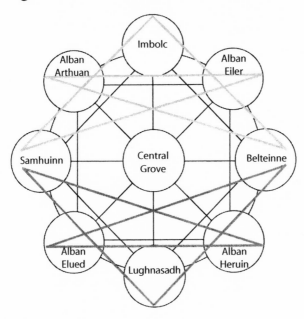

and so on around the wheel of the year. This has to be remembered in order to summon and banish the nwyfre of the Stations effectively.

In order to reach the point where you can shape nwyfre effectively through any of these symbols—the elements, pentagrams, Stations of the Wheel, or Ogham letters—you need to make the transition from theory to practice. This transition begins with basic magical exercises, the subject of the next chapter.

CHAPTER 3
The Essentials of Practice

One of the great obstacles to success in magic is also, paradoxically enough, one of the easiest to overcome. It unfolds from the common belief that the way to learn magic is to get hold of secret teachings most people don't have, either by opening the right book or finding the right teacher. This belief helps to sell books and boost the egos—and, often, the income—of teachers willing to cater to it, but it has nothing to do with the realities of learning magic. The secrets of magic have been public for centuries now, and yet the number of competent mages in the world has not gone up noticeably during that time.

Knowing secret teachings, in point of fact, will not make you a mage. The real secrets of magic are the same factors that bring success in any other human activity. This point has led more than one mage to argue that all human activities, without exception, are varieties of magic.

Imagine for a moment that instead of wanting to be a mage, you want to become a guitar player. You would not expect to reach that goal by announcing to your friends that you have become a guitar player, dressing like your favorite lead guitarist, reading plenty of books about guitar playing, buying guitars and leaving them around your home for visitors to admire, or attending concerts and listening to other people perform a few times a year. It never fails to amaze serious occultists how many people expect to become mages by doing the equivalent!

If you plan on becoming a guitarist, rather than just pretending to be one, three steps will get you from the desire to the reality. First, you need to decide what kind of music you want to play, and learn about its history and traditions, while picking up a good general knowledge of music theory. Second, you need to get a guitar and practice playing it every day, seven days a week, fifty-two weeks a year. Third, you need to learn from your practice, and to compare what you can do with what you want to do, not so you can puff up your ego or wallow in how bad you think you're failing, but so you can see what needs work and measure how your learning process is coming along.

These same three factors—knowledge, practice, and the ability to learn—are also the keys to magic. If you study magic, practice magic, and learn from your magical experiences, you'll become a competent mage. It really is as simple as that.

The art of ritual magic contains many different forms of practice, but three of them form the foundation for your training and development. The first is ritual itself, the second is divination, and the third is meditation. Think of them as the three legs that support the cauldron of Druid magic. The sooner you begin practicing these things, and weave them into your daily routine, the sooner the doors of Druid magic will open for you.

Ritual
The Sphere of Protection

In most traditional magical orders, the first step on the path of magical training consists of learning a simple ritual and practicing it regularly. To this day, new members of the Ancient Order of Druids in America (AODA) are taught such a ritual in the course of the Candidate grade, the very first initiation AODA offers. The same ritual, the Sphere of Protection, forms the foundation of ritual work in the system taught in this book and is central to the next two chapters.

The Sphere of Protection was created in the 1970s by Dr. John Gilbert, then one of the Order's archdruids, using material drawn from several older rituals. The version given here differs from his, and the version you will practice will most likely be different from the one written in this book. The reasons for this provide a useful lesson in how Druidry works.

Most magical systems require the student to use some fixed set of gods, symbols, and ideas. Because freedom of conscience is a core value in Druidry, however, Druid magic both encourages and requires a more personal approach. The Sphere of Protection accordingly uses whatever symbolism you find most evocative and powerful. The other side of this flexibility, of course, is that the instructions for this ritual can't be used like a recipe out of a cookbook. You need to put a certain amount of preparation and forethought in the Sphere of Protection before you can use it at all.

This will take time, and at least two other factors have the same effect. The first is that you need to commit the ritual to memory. This is a step that novices often try to avoid, but it has to be tackled, and the sooner the better. It just isn't possible to get the most out of magic while you're still fumbling with a book or a paper "cheat sheet," trying to figure out what comes next. Only after a ritual has been learned by heart, and practiced regularly until every stage of the work flows easily, does it become an effective tool in magic.

The other ingredient you need to put into the Sphere of Protection, and the other factor that takes time, is daily practice. This is another step that novices usually resist, but it's even more important than memorization. Think of it in the same terms as learning to play a guitar. No matter how much you read about guitar playing or how often you listen to other people's music on your CD player, if you want to learn how to play, you have to pick up the guitar and practice. It's easy to tell the difference between a guitarist who practices for an hour or so every day, and one who plays only when he feels like it, or when his friends come over to jam. Magic is exactly the same way, and mastering it takes time, effort, passion, and patience. If you only practice it now and then, don't expect to get past the garage-band level any time soon.

The Sphere has three phases: an opening, a closing, and a middle section in which the core work is done. The opening is called the Elemental Cross, the middle section is the Calling of the Elements, and the closing is the Circulation of Light. It's standard practice to learn the opening and closing first, and practice these together until the student can use them effectively as a container for the forces roused in the middle section. For this reason we'll leave the Calling of the Elements for later, and cover the Elemental Cross and Circulation of Light in this chapter.

If you belong to a Druid order that teaches a different basic ritual, or have learned some other ritual from books, you can use that in place of the Sphere of Protection. You will need to modify some of the other ceremonies given in this book, but every Druid mage invents his or her own workings sooner or later. Whatever basic ritual you choose, learn it, commit it to memory, and practice it daily. If you want to learn magic, there is no other way.

The Elemental Cross

Like every complete magical ritual, the Elemental Cross combines symbolism, gesture, voice, and imagination to formulate an intention. These aspects all take place at the same time when you perform the ritual. For the sake of clarity, however, I'll explain them one at a time, and many students find it best to work through them step-by-step in order.

Symbolism

The symbolic component of the Elemental Cross requires you to choose four expressions of spiritual power that, among them, define the universe for you. The traditional way is to choose two gods, one elder and one younger, and two goddesses, one elder and one younger. The two gods form a vertical axis, the elder above and the younger below; the two goddesses form a horizontal axis, the elder to the right and the younger to the left. You can vary this in whatever way works for you.

What if you're not comfortable invoking gods, saints, or any other personified spiritual power? The Sphere of Protection is flexible enough to handle impersonal symbols as well. Whatever symbols define your magical universe can be used for the Elemental Cross.

For example, when I perform the Sphere of Protection, I sometimes invoke four of the deities that play an important role in Druid Revival tradition: Hu the Mighty, the high god of Welsh Druid tradition; Hesus, the chief of tree spirits, who sits in the first fork of the sacred oak; Ceridwen, the old wise goddess of the sacred cauldron; and Niwalen, the young goddess of springtime greenery. At other times, when an impersonal approach works better for me, I invoke the sky above me, the land beneath me, the fire to my right hand and the water to my left.

A Druid who preferred to work with Irish deities might choose to invoke the Dagda, Lugh, Danu, and Brigid instead, while a Christian Druid might choose, from among the saints specially revered by the old Celtic Church, Saint Peter, Saint John the Evangelist, Saint Brigid, and Saint Mary Magdalene. One who prefers to work with animal powers might invoke the Hawk above, the Bear below, the Stag to the right, and the Salmon to the left. Druids with other beliefs may choose whatever divine powers appeal to them.

Gesture

The gestural component of the Elemental Cross includes physical orientation, stance, and hand movement. The physical orientation is based on the traditional lore of the four directions, and it varies depending on the intention guiding the ritual. As a daily practice, the Elemental Cross and Circulation of Light are traditionally done facing east, the direction of sunrise, which symbolizes inspiration and illumination. As part of a ritual working using the Grove Ritual, a ceremony covered later on in this book, the Elemental Cross and Circulation of Light are traditionally done facing south, the place of the Sun at its height. Feel free to experiment with these and other directions.

The stance is much less complex. Place your feet parallel to one another, with the length of one of your feet between them. Divide your weight evenly between your feet, and bend your knees very slightly, just enough to keep them from locking. Keep your spine upright but not stiff, as though you were suspended from the top of your head. Some stances used in other magical traditions close off the connections between your body and the nwyfre of the Earth; this one does just the opposite, since the Earth contacts are crucial in Druid magic.

The hand movements of this phase of the ritual trace out two lines, one vertical and one horizontal, crossing at the solar plexus—a point on your body just below your breastbone and above the pit of your stomach. They also focus attention on two points along the midline of the body, the solar plexus itself and the center of the forehead—the "third eye" center used in so many mystical disciplines. Originally this was done with a gesture like the Christian sign of the cross, but many people—including some Christians—prefer not to do this. The following movements get the same results without dragging in connotations that many people find inappropriate.

1. Stand straight but not stiff, your weight evenly divided between both feet and your arms at your sides. Take a moment to allow tension to drain out of your body and into the ground. Then, in a single smooth movement, raise your arms out to your sides and up, turning your palms upward. The arms and hands rise until your palms join above your head, fingertips pointing straight up. Next, draw your hands downward until your joined thumbs press against your forehead, and pause.

2. Bring your joined hands down below the level of your heart, fingertips still pointing up, and pause again with your joined thumbs pressed against your solar plexus. Pause here.

3. The next movement is a bit tricky, so follow closely. Leave the left hand exactly where it is, thumb against your body, fingertips pointing upward, palm facing to

the right. The right hand, however, moves out to the right, and ends up two feet or more past your right side, at or just below the level of your solar plexus, with the palm up and the fingers pointing out to your right. The right elbow remains bent. Glance to your right, as though looking along the line traced by the fingers of your right hand. Pause here.

4. Next, leave the right hand where it is and move the left hand in a mirroring motion, out to the left, ending two feet or so past your left side, at or just below the level of your solar plexus, with the palm up and the fingers pointing to your left. Your left elbow remains bent. Glance to your left, as though looking along the line traced by the fingers of your left hand. Pause here.

5. Then, in a single motion, extend both hands further out, straightening the arms, and turn your palms to face forward. At the end of this motion you are standing in the form of a cross, with both arms straight out to the sides, palms forward, body straight and balanced, and your gaze straight ahead. Pause in this position for a time, and then let your arms return gently to your sides. This completes the gesture component.

Voice

The vocal component of the Elemental Cross combines breath and speech to formulate the deities or symbols invoked in the practice. The words used in this phase of the ritual may be spoken in an ordinary voice, chanted, or sung.

1. As you raise your arms above your head, breathe in deeply, and continue to breathe in as you draw your joined hands to your forehead. As you pause with your hands against your forehead, say the name of the first

of the four powers you've chosen to invoke—the name of the elder god, if you're using the traditional approach. If you wish, add one or more titles to the name. For example, at this point in the ritual, I might say, "Hu the Mighty, great Druid god," or I might say, "By the sky above me."

2. Breathe in again as you lower your hands below your heart. As you pause with joined hands, say the name of the second power—the younger god, if you're following the traditional approach—along with any titles you find appropriate. For example, at this point in the ritual, I might say, "Hesus of the Oaks, chief of tree spirits," or I might say, "By the land beneath me."

3. Breathe in again as your right hand goes out to your right side. As you pause, say the name of the third power—the elder goddess, in the traditional approach—along with any titles you wish to use. For example, at this point I might say, "Ceridwen the Wise, keeper of the cauldron," or "By the fire to my right hand."

4. Breathe in again as your left hand goes out to your left side. As you pause, say the name of the fourth power—the younger goddess, in the traditional approach—along with any titles you wish to use. For example, at this point in the ritual, I might say, "Niwalen of the Flowers, child of spring," or "By the water to my left."

5. Breathe in again as your arms extend and your palms turn forward. As you pause, say a short prayer, invocation, or blessing appropriate to all four of the powers you have invoked. For example, at this point in the ritual, I say, "May the powers of nature bless and protect me, now and always." This completes the vocal component.

Imagination

The imaginal component of the Elemental Cross uses a specific set of images held in the mind during each phase of the ritual. The sort of inner work central to this component of magical practice is often called "visualization," but this term only touches one portion of the process, because imagination isn't limited to the visual dimension. People blind since birth, for example, often have powerful imaginations focused on the senses of sound and touch, and these can be just as effective in magic as the visual imagination that sighted people have. You'll find that when you hear and feel and smell and taste your mental imagery, as well as seeing it, the stronger and more vivid it will be, and the more effectively it will set nwyfre into motion.

Modern industrial culture distrusts and fears the human imagination, so it's no surprise that many people nowadays are convinced that they can't use it at all. A simple mental trick makes it easy to get past this limiting belief and use the mental gifts every human being has. Instead of trying to visualize something, simply imagine what it would look like if you *could* visualize it. The image in your mind of "what it would look like" is exactly what you're trying to achieve, and any defects in it will be cured with regular practice.

1. As you raise your hands above your head, imagine that the Sun is far above your head, radiating golden light downward toward you. As your hands join and descend to your forehead, imagine a ray of golden light descending to the crown of your head and passing within, to a point at the center of your head, where it forms a sphere of brilliant light a few inches across. Feel the warmth of the light radiating outward through your head. Hold this image as you invoke your first power.

2. As you bring your hands down to chest level, imagine that the ray of golden light descends further, creating a second sphere of brilliant light at your solar plexus. From there, as you invoke your second power, the ray extends straight down through the midline of your body into the ground beneath you, extending all the way down to the heart of the Earth. Visualize this as a brilliant sphere of silvery-green light, the color of sunlight on moving water, as large and bright as the Sun but located far below you.

3. As your right hand goes out to your right, imagine a second ray streaming out to the right from the sphere of light at your solar plexus, flowing through your right side and across the palm of your right hand in a straight line out to infinite distance. Hold this image as you invoke your third power.

4. As your left hand goes out to your left, imagine a third ray streaming out to the left from the sphere of light at your solar plexus, flowing through your left side and across the palm of your left hand in a straight line out to infinite distance. Hold this image as you invoke your fourth power. The pattern up to this point is shown in Figure 3-1.

5. As you extend your arms and turn your palms forward, imagine two more rays of light streaming out from the sphere at your solar plexus. One of them goes straight ahead of you into infinite distance, the other straight out behind you into infinite distance. At this point the sphere of light in your solar plexus is the meeting place of six rays of light extending above, below, to your left, to your right, ahead of you, and behind you. Hold this image as you say the final prayer, invocation, or blessing, then let the imagery fade from your mind. This completes the imaginal component.

Figure 3-1 The Elemental Cross

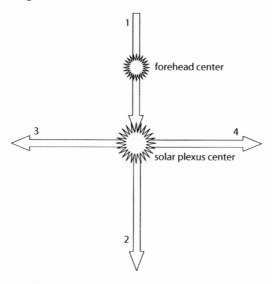

Intention

The intentional component of the Elemental Cross draws on the mythic image of the center of the world. Every traditional culture identified some spot on the Earth's surface as the center of all things, and oriented everything else in the world around it. For the Welsh, according to the tale of Lludd and Llevellys from the *Mabinogion,* it was in the vicinity of Oxford. For the Irish it was the Hill of Uisnech, where Mide, the Druid of the Milesians, kindled the first Belteinne fire. The ancient Greeks believed the center of the world was at Delphi; a classical myth told how Zeus released two eagles from opposite ends of the Earth at the same moment, flying toward one another, and they met in the air above Delphi. In the Middle Ages, Christians, Jews, and Muslims all identified Jerusalem as the exact center of the world, and the Stone of Foundation beneath the Dome of the Rock in Jerusalem was thought to be the first piece of solid ground to congeal out of primal chaos at the Creation.

These traditions have deep roots in the lore of Earth magic, for the subtle dance of nwyfre uniting people and the land comes into focus at certain places, and makes them centers where creative energy wells up from the depths. Still, what time and the Earth's own nwyfre do on a grand scale, magical ritual can do in a more focused and temporary way. A note in *Black Elk Speaks,* one of the classics of Native American spirituality, offers a key insight into this process. Comments John Neihardt, who took down the Lakota holy man's words, "Black Elk said the mountain he stood on in his vision was Harney Peak in the Black Hills. 'But anywhere is the center of the world,' he added" (Neihardt, 1988, p. 43).

Standing at the center of the world, in other words, is a condition of consciousness, not a matter of being in one place and not another. When you stand at the center of the world, as Black Elk and all the world's holy men and women have done, everything becomes visible to you because you stand at a point midway between every pair of opposites. East and west, north and south, above and below, and all the things symbolized by these directions, are all equally close and equally far away. Entering this state, the state of balance at the center of the world, is the intention of the Elemental Cross.

Of course, a single performance of a simple rite like this one won't get you to the place where all opposites come into balance, unless you're on the verge of getting there all by yourself. That's the point behind daily practice. As you formulate the intention of standing at the center of the world day after day, using the tools of symbolism, gesture, voice, and imagination to give it form, the intention becomes a point of contact where the three currents of Druid magic flow together and intention becomes reality.

The Circulation of Light

As the Elemental Cross begins the Sphere of Protection, the Circulation of Light completes it. This is not, strictly speaking, a complete ritual in itself, but simply takes the intention of the earlier phases of the ritual and extends it in space, using the imagination alone.

As soon as you finish the Elemental Cross, pause, and be aware of the sphere of light at your solar plexus. Then imagine the sphere enlarging until it surrounds you on all sides, extending out as far as you choose. With practice, you can make this any space you decide to protect—a room, a building, a valley, a bioregion, the entire Earth—but to begin with, make it a sphere around ten feet across, centered on your solar plexus and surrounding you on all sides. Pause again, concentrating on the image of the sphere of light around you, and concentrate on the idea that no hostile or unwanted influence can pass into the light from outside.

Once you have established this image solidly, the next step is to spin the sphere around you in three different directions. This can be tricky to picture mentally, so it's often useful to get a ball—any size will do—and try out the motions with the ball first. Figure 3-2 shows the three rotations of the sphere, as though they were being done by someone facing you. The first one goes over your head, down in front, under your feet and up the back; the second goes around from left to right in front, and from right to left behind you; the third goes from above down to your right, under your feet, and then up to your left.

The trick is to start with the first rotation, add the second without stopping the first, and then add the third while keeping the other two going. This is where the ball comes in handy as a help to your imagination. Hold your hands in front of you, level with each other, with the ball poised

Figure 3-2 Three Rotations

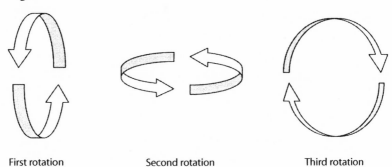

First rotation   Second rotation   Third rotation

between your two index fingers so it can spin freely. Start the ball spinning by pushing up with your thumbs against the side of the ball nearest you. This is the first rotation.

Next, imagine that the ball is the Earth and you're the Moon. Walk around the ball in a clockwise circle, leaving it at the center of the circle, while keeping it spinning between your index fingers by pushing up with your thumbs. Now the ball is spinning in two directions at once—over and under, moved by your thumbs, and around from left to right, moved by your feet. Those are the first two rotations.

Now, while you keep the ball spinning and keep walking around it in a circle, move your left index finger up and your right index finger down, turning the ball over as it spins. Unless you're double-jointed, you won't be able to take it past half a turn, but imagine that it keeps on turning over and over, left to right, as it spins in the two other directions. Once you have the image, put the ball away, and get ready to do the same thing with energy.

Start where you left off, with the sphere of light surrounding you. Just like the ball, it begins to rotate the first way, up from behind and down from in front. Make the motion slow at first, and then gradually speed it up until the sphere is whirling around you in a blur of speed.

Keep it spinning, and then add the second rotation, just as you did with the ball by walking in a circle around it. Imagine it moving slowly at first, then faster and faster, until the second rotation also becomes a blur of speed. Then add the third rotation, as you did by moving your index fingers, slowly at first again and then faster and faster, until you see yourself surrounded by a sphere of white light spinning in all directions at once. Imagine all three rotations reaching infinite speed, so that the sphere around you appears to be perfectly still.

This final stillness concludes the ritual. You can make a closing gesture at this point—for example, crossing your arms in front of your chest and saying something on the order of "I thank the powers for their blessings"—or not, as you prefer. Pause for a moment, and notice how the space around you feels. At first you may not notice much, but with time and regular practice this will change. Pay attention to what you perceive, and note how changes in the way you do the ritual affect the way the space feels afterward.

Divination

Divination, the second leg of the cauldron of Druid magic, takes many forms. Of the dozens of methods of divination practiced in the Druid community today, most would have been completely unfamiliar not only to the ancient Druids but to the founders of the Druid Revival as well. This is an excellent sign, as it shows that Druidry is alive and growing from its deep roots.

One system the old Druids might have recognized, however, is based on the Ogham alphabet. Reintroduced to the Pagan community by Colin Murray in the late twentieth century, Ogham divination has become a popular art in the modern Druid community, and it has much to offer the Druid mage in training—not least because anything that will help you become more familiar with Ogham will make it easier for you to use the fews in magic.

To practice Ogham divination, you'll need twenty-five cards or sticks that can be marked with the Ogham fews; sticks are more traditional, but many people prefer cards because they are easier to handle. You can purchase several different versions of Ogham cards, and many Pagan stores now sell Ogham sticks as well; you can also make either one. In either case, if you make a set, be sure you have a way of telling when the few is upright and when it's reversed, since this makes a difference in divination. A spot of black ink on the bottom of each Ogham stick will do, and for cards, writing the name of each few on the top of its card works well.

Like ritual, divination should be practiced every day, and a basic three-few spread does well for this purpose. Shuffle the sticks or cards thoroughly, and then deal out three in the form of the Three Rays of Light, one of the classic Druid symbols, as shown in Figure 3-3. The first few goes on the left, the place of the Ray of Knowledge; it represents what comes

Figure 3-3   The Three Rays of Light (Basic Ogham Reading)

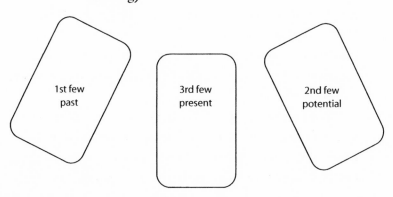

1st few
past

3rd few
present

2nd few
potential

to the situation from the past. The second goes on the right, the place of the Ray of Power; it represents the potentials for change in the situation, and leads into the future. The third goes at the center, the place of the Ray of Peace; it represents your position in the present, between past and future.

Turning three Ogham fews into a meaningful reading takes practice, and this is one of the reasons why daily practice is so important. Even with practice, interpreting the reading is the difficult part of divination for many people, but it doesn't have to be that way.

One of the chief obstacles to interpretation is the idea that each symbol in the divinatory alphabet has to have one and only one meaning. The process becomes much easier when you remember that the symbols of a divination system are as many faceted as the images of dreams. The following notes on the meanings of the Ogham alphabet should be treated as a starting point for your own intuition, not as a cage that restricts what the card can mean. It can help to look at the meanings listed and ask yourself, "What does this make me think of? What does this bring to mind?" Pay attention to the answers that surface, no matter how strange they may seem.

One very effective way to learn divination, with Ogham or any other oracle, is to ask the same simple question each day—"What do I most need to know about the day before me?"—and write down your interpretation of the reading. Go back a day later and compare the symbols you cast, and the interpretation you gave to them, with the events of the day. With time and regular practice, this process will teach you the meanings each of the Ogham fews have for you, and help guide the growth of your own intuitive abilities.

Can you use another divination system instead of Ogham? Of course, but Ogham is more than just an oracle.

What the Hebrew alphabet is to Cabalistic magic and the runes are to Norse magic, the Ogham is to Druid magic. Many of the magical methods given in later chapters rely on the fews. Use them for divination, and you'll find that they and their meanings stick in the memory much more quickly.

Divinatory Meanings of the Fews

BEITH

Upright meaning: Beginnings, new possibilities, potentials. Renewal and rebirth. A favorable sign in most matters, though there may be discomforts involved. *Reversed meaning:* Blind alleys, wasted effort. Creative blockages. Remaining fixated on the past, or on things that have been lost. Longing for the impossible.

LUIS

Upright meaning: Clarity and attention to details. Concentration on the task at hand. Purification. Danger avoided or overcome. A choice between two paths. *Reversed meaning:* Confusion, uncertainty, deception, delusion. Lack of defenses. Something is not what it appears to be. Someone may be misleading you— possibly yourself.

NUIN

Upright meaning: Connection and transformation. Relationship to a larger context. You are part of a wider world. Events may be more important than they appear. *Reversed meaning:* Isolation and self-containment. You are separated from what is going on, for good or ill. Boredom and lack of initiative may blind you to possibilities in the present.

FEARN

Upright meaning: Protection and guidance, a bridge over deep waters. Steadfastness. Good advice received from others or your own inner depths. Spiritual guidance and insight, the presence of the gods. An unexpected way past a difficulty.

Reversed meaning: Willful blindness, refusal to listen to advice. Arrogance and lack of insight. You are out of your depth.

SAILLE

Upright meaning: Moving with the flow of events. Intuition, dreaming, the unconscious. Letting go of fixed ideas and responding to the moment. Faith in a personal vision.

Reversed meaning: Inability to move with the situation due to rigidity, confusion, or lack of awareness. Unforeseen dangers. A difficult time, which will pass eventually.

HUATH

Upright meaning: Patience, reserve, retreat. A time of waiting and planning rather than action. Obstacles that can be overcome. Success after a delay. Temporary obstacles.

Reversed meaning: Inappropriate action, rushing ahead when patience and planning are called for. A risk of failure. You need to stop and reconsider.

DUIR

Upright meaning: Success, forward movement, attainment. Power and energy; you have all you need to accomplish your goals. A door opens in the outer world.

Reversed meaning: Help from those in positions of power or authority. Success despite inadequate means. Borrowed strength. A gift.

TINNE

Upright meaning: Conflict, challenge, struggle against opposing forces. Victory against the odds. A change of fortune. Decisive action is favored.

Reversed meaning: Inadequate strength or skill, the possibility of defeat. Lack of direction and balance. You need to build your strength and understand the nature of the opposition.

COLL

Upright meaning: Knowledge, intelligence, talent. Transformation and flexibility. The beginning of a new stage in life. Learning. Communication and teaching, new information.

Reversed meaning: Creative and intellectual blockages, lack of insight. Often, fear of failure, leading to a retreat to familiar ground.

QUERT

Upright meaning: Happiness, healing, and recovery. Awakenings and new experiences. An unexpected gift. The rewards of success. An opportunity to live more fully.

Reversed meaning: An unavoidable choice among alternatives. Mixed gain and loss. A temptation to scattered effort or procrastination that must be overcome.

MUIN

Upright meaning: Inspiration and prophecy. Community. The influence of spiritual factors on the situation. Unexpected truths. Freedom from limits and restrictions.

Reversed meaning: Burdens, difficulties. A need to relax and unwind. You have been trying too hard in unproductive ways.

GORT

Upright meaning: Slow and indirect progress, movement by roundabout paths. Purpose, determination, self-control. A difficult but viable path.

Reversed meaning: Entanglement in circumstances, or in your own egotism. Think twice about what you are doing, and why.

NGETAL

Upright meaning: Swiftness, sudden movement, instability. Healing, change for the better. A message or an opportunity. You are not yet finished with your work.

Reversed meaning: Stuckness, inability to act. A need for healing. Patience. You are not yet ready to begin.

STRAIF

Upright meaning: Necessity and inevitability. The hard realities of life. Something that cannot be changed. The results of one's own actions. The influence of fate.

Reversed meaning: Pain, difficulty, retribution, unavoidable suffering. A difficult path that must be taken. Every choice leads to unhappiness.

RUIS

Upright meaning: Healing, resolution, completion. Transitions from one state of being to another. Difficulties permanently overcome. An omen of success in most things.

Reversed meaning: Endings and departures. The need to release things that are past their time. Facing up to facts. Embarrassment and shame. Illness and disability.

AILM

Upright meaning: Insight, transformation, expanded awareness. Change for the better. The ability to see things in perspective. Peak experiences, dreams and visions.

Reversed meaning: Lack of perspective, ignorance of the broader picture. Unrealistic ideas. You need to step back and assess the situation more carefully.

ONN

Upright meaning: Gathering together, combination of forces. Energy, life, vigor, sexuality and attraction. Opportunities, though not without potential problems.

Reversed meaning: Difficulties and delays, overconfidence. Desires out of touch with the realities of the situation. Uncoordinated efforts. Problems, but with potential benefits.

UR

Upright meaning: Spiritual power, the forces of nature. Fulfillment. The coming of new life. A door opens in the inner world. Passion, power, and magic. Creation.

Reversed meaning: Weakness, dispersed energies, loss of contact with nature and the spirit. Dreamy neglect of realities. A need for recuperation and reconnection.

EADHA

Upright meaning: Courage and tenacity in the face of opposition. A struggle in which victory is possible but not certain. A quest for inner strength.

Reversed meaning: Declining strength. Compromise and negotiation. Prudence. If you continue in your present path the results will not be good.

IOHO

Upright meaning: Enduring realities, that which remains unchanged. Old age, legacies from the past. The consequences of present actions.

Reversed meaning: Stagnation and immobility. Things lingering past their time. The past as a burden not yet overcome.

KOAD

Upright meaning: Complexity, the presence of many factors. Capacity for freedom. A place of balance from which many possibilities open.

Reversed meaning: Confusion and bewilderment. There may be too many factors at work to allow successful prediction.

OIR

Upright meaning: Radical transformation, the flash of the lightning bolt. Sudden change, illumination or destruction, set in motion by forces outside the situation.

Reversed meaning: Patience and preparation. The path before you is slow and cannot be hurried. Wait for outside forces to act.

UILLEAND
Upright meaning: Secrets and revelations, the influence of the subtle and seemingly insignificant. Small causes with large effects. Insight into the nature of the situation.
Reversed meaning: Situation is not what it seems. Hidden factors are a source of complications. The information you need is not available to you.

PHAGOS
Upright meaning: Knowledge and lore, learning, study, education. The wisdom of the past as a guide to the present and future.
Reversed meaning: Ignorance. Lack of attention to existing knowledge. Failure to learn from experience.

MÓR
Upright meaning: Unexpected change, the arrival of a new influence. The effects of destiny.
Reversed meaning: Sudden endings and disruptions, the dissolution of the familiar.

Meditation

Meditation, the third leg of the cauldron of Druid magic, also provides the Druid path as a whole with its core inner practice. Nearly all the traditional Druid orders teach some kind of meditation, and most expect students to practice it regularly. The daily experience of turning inward in meditation is essential to the Druid path of nature spirituality, since it brings you into contact with the part of nature closest to you—the nature of your own body, enaid, and mind. As Philip Carr-Gomm reminds us in his inspiring book, *The Druid Way,* "Nature isn't only out there!"

Any form of meditation that directs attention inward, toward your own inner life and experience, makes a valuable part of a Druid path. The particular form of meditation taught and practiced in AODA and many other traditional Druid orders, however, fits particularly well with the needs of Druidry as well as those of Druid magic. The basics of this method can be summed up in a few pages, and this is what I have done here; a more complete discussion appears in *The Druidry Handbook.*

The most important detail about this method is also the easiest part to describe. Most of the methods of meditation practiced in the Western world nowadays teach the student to stop thinking entirely by chanting a mantra, focusing on breathing or the body, concentrating on thought-stopping paradoxes, or some similar tactic. These methods can get you to mystical states of consciousness, but shutting down the mind has its drawbacks as well. Too often people who pursue such methods intensively reach impressive spiritual states, but lose their ability to think clearly or deal with life in the ordinary world.

From a Druid perspective, thinking is natural to human beings, and trying to get rid of what is natural is always a mistake. Thus Druid meditation focuses on training the mind and harmonizing it with the rest of the self, not on shutting it down. This is done by directing the mind toward a previously chosen image or idea, called the "theme" of the meditation. After some simple preparations, the meditator explores the theme in thought, restraining the mind whenever it tries to stray from the theme but giving it free rein to follow the theme as far as it can. This kind of meditation is called "discursive meditation," because it often takes the form of an inner discourse or dialogue as the mind works with the subject matter given by the theme.

This sort of meditation has the same benefits as any other method of meditation—it clears and centers your mind, relaxes and heals your body, and teaches you to shape your own inner life rather than being pushed around passively by it—but it has another benefit most others lack. Most occult traditions in the Western world use enigmatic images, symbols, and texts to conceal the deeper dimensions of their teachings. These are meant to be "unpacked" through discursive meditation, and they give up their secrets in no other way. Once you learn to meditate in this way, you have the key to most traditional occult lore.

The best way to harvest themes for meditation is to note down ideas and images that catch your attention, because they suggest interesting possibilities to you or because you can't figure them out at all. The minor themes are often just as important as the big ones. Beginners often choose big themes and either flounder about or skate over the surface, missing the potential depths of the practice. As a general rule, if your theme takes more than a short sentence to describe, it's too large for a single meditation and should be broken up into smaller bits, then put together later on.

Posture and Practical Issues

Start meditation practice by sitting down on a chair with a plain, cushionless seat. Sit far enough forward on it that your lower back isn't resting against the back of the chair. Your feet should be flat on the floor. Straighten your back without stiffening it, and hold your head upright, without letting it slump forward. Your hands rest palm down on your thighs, and your elbows are at your sides. This posture for meditation, unlike the cross-legged positions common in Eastern systems of meditation, doesn't seal your energies off from the rest of the cosmos. As Druids, we always participate in the dance of energies through the wider world.

Most people find it useful to meditate in the same place each day, and at the same time of day or the same point in the daily cycle for those who have variable schedules—right before breakfast, say. An outdoor setting is best, when weather and circumstances permit, but a corner of your bedroom or some other convenient indoor place will do nearly as well. If you can do so, meditate facing east, facing into the currents of energy flowing through the subtle body of the Earth; this is good for health and also helps develop the mind. A clock placed so that you can see it without moving your head completes the setting.

Meditation practice consists of three stages, which should be learned one at a time. Start out doing only the first stage, relaxation, in your daily meditation practice, and continue at that level until you feel that you have a good sense of the technique. Then add the next stage, breathing, and continue practicing relaxation and breathing each day until both of them feel familiar and comfortable. Only then go on to the third stage, meditation itself.

Relaxation Stage

Start each practice by settling into the meditation position, and then consciously relax each part of your body, starting with your head and moving step-by-step down to the soles of your feet. Let the tensions drain downward, like water, and imagine them flowing out through your feet into the Earth, which absorbs them and transforms them into energy. Leave your body with only the muscular tensions you need to stay sitting up. Take as much time at this as you wish. The more muscular tension you can release, the easier and more productive your meditation practice will be.

Practice relaxation by itself until your body feels comfortably poised as soon as you settle into your meditation posture and begin relaxing. At that point, add the next stage.

Breathing Stage

After going through the process of relaxation, spend a few minutes paying conscious attention to your breath, breathing in and out slowly, evenly, and fully. A traditional breathing exercise called the "Rhythmic Breath" is commonly used here. Breathe slowly in while counting slowly and silently from one to three; hold your breath in, while counting from one to three; breathe out, counting from one to three; and hold the breath out, with the lungs empty, while counting from one to three, and repeat. The counts should all be at the same pace, and the breath should be held in or out with the muscles of the chest and diaphragm. Don't shut your throat during this practice, as this can lead to lung problems.

Practice relaxation, followed by breathing, as your daily meditation practice until the rhythm of the Rhythmic Breath becomes automatic and you can remain comfortably relaxed for five minutes of breathing. At that point, add the third stage.

Meditation Stage

After relaxation and five minutes or so of rhythmic breathing, turn your attention to the theme of the meditation. State the theme silently to yourself in a few words, or visualize it before you in a single image. Hold it in your mind for a short time, and then start thinking about it, turning it over and over in your mind, exploring its implications and connections. Choose one of these that appeals to you, and follow it out as far as you can. Keep working at it for the period of time you choose for your meditation—ten minutes is good to start with—and then pay attention to your breathing or practice the Rhythmic Breath again for a minute or so to help make the transition back to ordinary awareness.

When your thoughts veer from the theme during meditation, as they almost certainly will in the early stages of training, don't simply yank them back to the theme. Instead, follow your straying thoughts back to the point where they left the train of thought you were following, and proceed from there. If you started out meditating on the Sphere of Protection and ended up thinking about Aunt Martha's tortilla casserole, say, ask yourself what you were thinking about just before the casserole came to mind. If it was Aunt Martha, what came before that? Her apartment, of course, where a little statue in her china hutch came to mind when you were trying to think about the Welsh goddess Elen, the young goddess you invoke in the Sphere of Protection. Over time, this habit of tracing back your thoughts will teach your mind to return to your theme as readily as it strays from it.

Meditation should be practiced every day. Once you've learned all three phases of the practice, five minutes of relaxation, five minutes of breathing, and ten minutes of actual meditation makes a good session for beginners. Add more time gradually, as you learn how to keep your mind focused for longer and longer intervals.

The Druid Journal

All the practices in this book should be recorded in your Druid journal. What is a Druid journal? Simply a notebook in which you keep details of your practices, workings and magical experiences. A sample might run like this:

January 19th, 2008

6:30 AM, morning meditation, 10 minutes. Theme was the quote from Morris Berman in the first chapter. I tried to see the connection between disenchantment and the ecological crisis, and realized just how deeply the notion of the world as dead matter and raw material is woven into modern thought. Mental focus was shaky at first but I managed to get it under control after a little while.

7:08 AM, morning divination. Ngetal reversed, Koad, Beith. I feel stuck in my current situation, but with appropriate guidance and patience I can make a new beginning.

7:10 PM, Sphere of Protection. Fairly strong. For the first time I got a definite sense of standing at the center of the world—just a glimpse, probably, but it was pretty intense.

Many magical and Druid orders require their initiates to keep a journal as part of their training program, and AODA is among them. A journal is one good way to encourage people to do the course work regularly, and an order that requires students to pass an examination before they go on to the next degree, as AODA does, can have students go back into their journals and pull out details of their work for the examination. Too often, though, this comes to be seen as the entire point of keeping a magical journal, and the real value of the exercise gets lost.

The key to using a magical journal is that it allows you to check your memory against an objective record. This is partly a way of sidestepping problems with selective memory. In magical training, as in anything else, memory bends to suit the needs of the ego. For example, if you skip practices more often than not, selective memory can still convince you that you're hard at work on your magical training. Your Druid journal can tell you otherwise.

Your Druid journal also provides a record of magical experiences, and these eventually become one of the most important resources you have in magical training. It often happens that in magical states of consciousness, the mage receives occult symbols, teachings, and techniques. Most of the material that fills the pages of textbooks of magic today started out as entries in someone's journal. Your magical journal can serve the same purpose. This is why you should copy down the details of each practice while they're still fresh in your memory, before the details have slipped away, and why you should copy down everything, not just what seems important at the time. A week, a month, or a year later, the detail that didn't seem important at the time may turn out to be the key to new realms of magic.

PART TWO
The Practice of Druid Magic

CHAPTER 4
The Gates of the Elements

Learning and practicing the exercises in chapter 3 will build a firm foundation for the rest of your magical work. The first step beyond the basics starts, ironically enough, by returning to one of them. The Sphere of Protection ritual contains a middle section, the Calling of the Elements, that you should learn and practice once you can do the Elemental Cross and Circulation of Light easily and effectively from memory.

The Calling of the Elements consists of seven separate parts, working with the seven elements of air, water, fire, earth, spirit above, spirit below, and spirit within. The ritual calls for you to invoke all seven elements, and banish the unbalanced aspects of four of them. *Invoke* literally means "call in," and *banish* means to send away. In terms of the theory of magic introduced back in chapter 1, to invoke is to fill the nwyfre of your own enaid with the resonance of a symbol, and to banish is to close your enaid against a symbol so that it finds no response in you. This is one of the essential skills of practical magic; it builds abilities you can put to use in many other ways.

Invoking and Banishing
by the First Gate

Like the Elemental Cross, each of the seven invocations and four banishings in the Sphere of Protection ritual combines symbolism, gesture, voice, and imagination to formulate an intention. In this first Gate, we'll go through them one at a time.

Symbolism

In the traditions of modern Druidry, the eastern quarter of the world is above all else the place where the Sun rises, and this symbolism of light spills over into air, the element assigned to the east. Morning, springtime, and every other image of newborn light and life correspond to this Gate, and so does inspiration and illumination of every kind. Another symbol of air is the one shown here: a circle with a line extending up from its top. This represents air being born from the infinite potential of spirit.

Gesture

Face east. Using the first two fingers of your right hand, trace the symbol of air in front of you. Start where the circle joins the line, tracing the circle in a clockwise direction, and then trace the upward line. This is the invoking form of the symbol. Hold your hand still for a time, and then trace the symbol of air in its banishing form; first trace the circle in a *counterclockwise* direction, and then draw the upward line.

Voice

Like the Elemental Cross, the invocations and banishings in the Calling of the Elements can and should be changed to use the symbols that define the universe for you. If you are comfortable working with gods and goddesses, or other person-alized spiritual powers, choose one that corresponds to the element of air.

In the Welsh Druid lore that provides so much of the magical symbolism in modern Druidry, the god Hu the Mighty fills this role. The "Great Druid God" of AODA tra-dition, Hu is the active power of divine creation in the world. His name is pronounced with the Welsh *u;* to pro-nounce this, purse your lips as though you meant to say "ooooh," and then—without changing the position of your lips—try to say "eeee" instead. An Irish god appropriate to this element is Aengus Og (pronounced "AHN-gus OHG"), the youthful god of love and life, while Christian Druids usu-ally invoke Saint Raphael the Archangel as the regent of air.

These names can be spoken in the ordinary way, but what occultists call "vibration" makes a more magically effec-tive method. Vibration, in occult jargon, is a special way of chanting magically powerful names and words. To learn it, try it with a simple vowel tone like "ah" or "oh." Draw in a deep breath, and chant the sound, stretching it out until you run out of breath. As you make the sound, try changing the shape of your mouth and the quality of the tone until you get a buzzing or tingling feeling in your throat and chest, or else-where in your body. The effect may be slight at first, but practice will make it stronger. It will also bring the ability to focus the vibration at various points of the body, and in time to focus it outside the body as well.

In ritual work, vibrate the name of the god, angel, or other spiritual being ruling the element or other symbolic pattern you invoke, and speak any other words you wish to use in a more ordinary voice. For example, invoking air in the east, I say, "By the hawk of May in the heights of morning, and in the great name Hu, I invoke the air, its gods, its spirits and its powers." The name of Hu is the only word I vibrate, and I extend it to a full breath, letting the vibration resonate all through my enaid. I then say, "May I receive the blessings of air," and when I receive those blessings, I say, "I thank the air for its gifts." When banishing, I say, "And with the help of the powers of air, I banish from within me and around me all unbalanced manifestations of air. I banish them far away from me."

If you prefer to invoke the elements in an impersonal form, simply leave out the divine name and the vibration. While invoking, for example, you can say words like these: "By the hawk of May in the heights of morning, I invoke the air, its gods, its spirits, and its powers. May I receive the blessings of air this day." Pause to receive the blessings, then say, "I thank the air for its gifts." When banishing, say words like these: "And with the help of the powers of air, I banish from within me and around me all unbalanced manifestations of air. I banish them far away from me."

Imagination

As you trace the invoking air symbol, imagine that your fingers are drawing it in the air in front of you in brilliant yellow flame. When you finish and point to the center, imagine the circle filled with paler, transparent yellow flame. Then, as you speak the words invoking the powers and blessings of air, concentrate on air. Picture before you a morning sky, modeling the image on what dawn looks like in the land where you live. Feel the wind and smell the fresh morning air, again using your memories of real mornings. As you imagine this, feel the powers and blessings of air flowing into you. Imagine that the yellow light of air flows into your body through your solar plexus, and feel that you have become so light and nimble that you could dance on the winds.

When you thank the air and trace the banishing form of the symbol, release the imagery of air. Concentrate on the idea that all airy imbalances in your life are swept away by the winds and lost in the vastness of the skies. Take as much time as you need on this visualization.

Intention

The basic intention of each of the seven invocations and four banishings in the Calling of the Elements is the same. When you invoke, you attune your enaid to one of seven great symbolic patterns and take on its qualities. These are the blessings you call into yourself. When you banish, you define the way your enaid participates in the elemental pattern to remove all unbalanced and harmful influences from yourself and your life, sending them back to their proper place in the cycle of things.

You don't need to force the element to do these things, and it's a serious mistake to think of magic in terms of commanding and forcing nwyfre to obey you. The seven elements aren't entities outside you that need to be controlled. Equally, they aren't parts of yourself that you can boss around. Instead, the elements are relationships that connect you with the world. When you invoke, you simply attune your enaid to focus on a particular set of relationships, then set that corresponds to one of the elements. When you banish, you use that relationship to redefine the problematic parts of your life. The ritual itself expresses these intentions, and trying to make the intentions happen by willpower is like trying to make a river flow faster by pushing the water.

For the next two or three weeks, include this section in your daily practice. Perform the Elemental Cross, then invoke and banish by air, then perform the Circulation of Light. Practice it until you have this phase of the ritual by heart, and can feel the air respond to the ritual. During the time you spend on this, pay attention to any symbols relating to air that show up in other aspects of your life. You can also work with air using the following method.

Receptive Working

Air in all its different moods and movements forms a reservoir of nwyfre on which you can draw. Choose a condition of the air that expresses a quality you would like to develop in yourself. If you have a hard time settling your mind and centering yourself, choose the still air before sunrise; if you feel that you lack strength, choose a time of strong wind; if you feel burdened and stuck in a rut, choose a time when the breeze is light and dancing, and so on.

When the air has the quality you need, go outside and stand in a place where there is as much open air as possible around you. If the wind is blowing, face into it; otherwise, face east. Focus your attention on your solar plexus. This area is to magical energies what the nose and mouth are to physical air. You breathe energies in and out through your solar plexus all the time without noticing it. This practice teaches you to notice it and make use of it.

Imagine, as you stand there in the open air, that you are drawing the quality you need out of the air into yourself with each breath. If you're seeking stillness, and you're standing outside in the perfectly still air of a winter dawn, imagine that with each breath you draw in, you draw stillness in through the solar plexus. As you breathe out, imagine that stillness spreads out from the solar plexus to fill your whole body. Do this three or nine times, concentrating on what you are doing, then thank the powers of air in your own words. This completes the exercise.

Active Working

When the air doesn't express the quality you wish to develop in yourself, you can charge the air with your intention and then breathe it into yourself. Do this by imagining the air around you filled with a color that expresses your intention, as given in Table 4-1. This color helps to anchor a mood or feeling, and the mood or feeling combines with the spoken intention to bring you into resonance with patterns in the nwyfre that will help you accomplish your goal.

Table 4-1   Color Symbolism

Red   is energizing and awakening, and heightens the body's vitality. Use it whenever you need strength, courage, and vital power.

Orange   combines red's energy with yellow's clarity; it gives focus and precision, and balances the nervous system. Use it to direct and strengthen the mind.

Yellow   is balancing and uplifting, and brings clarity to the mind and spirit. Use it to banish depression and summon inspiration.

Green   combines yellow's clarity with blue's receptivity; it fosters growth and healing, and helps calm the digestive system. Use it for healing and creativity of all kinds, and also for financial and economic issues.

Blue   is passive and receptive, opening the doors of awareness to a wider world. Use it to heighten intuition and perception, and to work with dreams.

Violet   combines active red and receptive blue; it is the color of power, and awakens psychic and artistic gifts. Use it to find and express your talents.

White   is the color of pure spirit and unites all the other colors. Use it for spiritual development of all kinds.

Before you perform the ritual, work out a single word or phrase or, at most, a short and simple sentence that expresses your intention. To help yourself focus your mind more clearly in meditation, for example, you might use "clarity," "perfect focus," or "My mind is clear of unwanted thoughts." Take your time, think through the implications of what you want, and stay clear of ambiguity. One of the rules of magic is that you get what you ask for, whether or not what you ask for is what you actually want! It's also best to phrase an intention as a statement of the situation you desire, in the present tense—"My mind is clear" rather than "My mind will be clear" or "I want my mind to be clear"—so that your intentionality focuses on a present reality, not a hope for the future or an unfulfilled desire.

For now, choose an intention that involves shaping your thoughts, feelings, or attitudes rather than your physical body or anything outside yourself. Magic can transform anything in the universe of human experience, but it takes practice and a fair amount of skill to get definite results when working magic on physical matter or other people's minds. Working magic on yourself is easier at first, and the results usually make themselves known to you sooner and more dramatically, too. Later on, when you've built skill and confidence, you can reach further.

Once you have chosen your intention, imagine that the air around you is filled with the color that corresponds to the intention most closely. Repeat the purpose silently three times, imagining it echoing through the air around you, and imagine that the air around you becomes an ocean of the appropriate color—in this case, yellow, the color of clarity. At the same time, imagine it filled with a mood or feeling appropriate to your intention—in this case, with a sense of perfect stillness and clarity.

Then imagine that you're breathing the yellow light and the clarity into your body with each inbreath, and breathing it out with each outbreath, through your solar plexus. As you breathe in, imagine the color and the feeling flowing into your body and filling it completely, so your whole body glows with the color. As you breathe out, imagine every trace of the color and mood flowing out of you, so your body is empty of both, but the space around you is filled with them. Do this for as long as you wish.

One useful application of this technique is as a preliminary step for meditation. While doing the rhythmic breath, imagine yourself breathing in and out an appropriate color. Pale orange and yellow are the colors most often used for this, because they foster calm and concentration. Give them a try and see how they affect your meditation practice.

Invoking and Banishing
by the Second Gate

This is the second invocation and banishing, done after you invoke and banish air, and it follows the same pattern as the first.

Water in the Druid tradition has meanings not shared by other magical systems. Wisdom in the old Celtic lore is symbolized by a salmon who dwells in a sacred pool. To Druids, water is the element of learning, growth, and development, and it also has close symbolic connections to trees and other growing things. If air is the flash of inspiration that awakens the mind, water is the growth of wisdom through study, practice, and reflection. Its symbol is the triangle pointing down, representing water's downward movement.

To invoke and banish by water, turn to the west. With the first two fingers of your right hand trace a triangle with one point down, as shown in figure, starting at the bottom point and tracing clockwise. Visualize it in blue flame, and then fill it with paler, transparent blue flame. Then say words like these: "By the salmon of wisdom who dwells in the sacred pool, and in the great name Esus, I invoke the water, its gods, its spirits, and its powers. May I receive the blessings of water this day." Esus was originally a god of the Celts of Gaul, and almost nothing is known nowadays about him or the traditions surrounding him. Back in the nineteenth century, however, Druids began invoking Esus as the chief of all tree spirits, a god of wisdom who sits in the first fork of the sacred oak. This is how he is invoked here; his name is pronounced "EH-suus," with the Welsh *u* again. If you prefer an Irish god, invoke Manannan, the Irish sea god; his name is pronounced "mah-NAHN-un." If you prefer Christian symbolism, Saint Gabriel the archangel is invoked in this quarter, and if you prefer not to work with personal powers, of course, simply leave out any name.

Pause for a time, and concentrate on water. Imagine the largest natural body of water in the region where you live. If you live on the seacoast, imagine the ocean reaching out in front of you; if you live near a lake or river, imagine that; if you live in the desert, and water appears only in springs in rock clefts, imagine one of these. Weave the sounds of water, whether those are rolling waves or the trickling of a spring, and the scents of water into your imagery. As you picture all this, feel the powers and blessings of water flowing into you through your solar plexus. Imagine your body filled with the blue light of water, and feel yourself becoming so fluid and responsive that nothing can contain or restrict you.

Then say, "I thank the water for its gifts," and trace the symbol counterclockwise, again from the bottom of the triangle. Say words like the following: "And with the help of the powers of water, I banish from within me and around me all unbalanced manifestations of water. I banish them far away from me." Concentrate on the idea that all unbalanced factors in your life are swept away and drowned in the depths. Take as much time as you need on this visualization.

For the next two or three weeks, include this section in your daily practice: perform the Elemental Cross, then invoke and banish by air, then invoke and banish by water, then perform the Circulation of Light. Practice it until you have this phase of the ritual by heart, and can feel the water respond to the ritual. During the time you spend doing this, pay attention to any of the symbols of the Gate of Water that show up in other aspects of your life. You can also work with the realm of water by using the following methods.

Receptive Working

The waters of the world provide a reservoir of nwyfre that can be used in your work as a Druid mage. For countless centuries, peoples around the world have recognized certain springs and other water sources as specially sacred. If you have access to one or more traditionally sacred sources of water, or know a source of water that seems sacred to you, you can use the water for a wide range of magical purposes. Drinking the water from such a place, bathing in it, or laving (washing a part of your body, such as the third eye center in your forehead) with it, can amplify your spiritual development. When you use the water in one of these ways, clear your mind of thoughts and simply be aware of the water as clearly as possible. Allow its energies to work in their own way.

Water also absorbs nwyfre from other sources, and you can use it to purify yourself or anything else by washing. Cold water—as close as possible to 39°F, the temperature at which water absorbs nwyfre most effectively—is best for this purpose. If you spend time around people or places that make you uncomfortable, washing with cold water is a good way to clear away the unwanted nwyfre and the moods or emotional states it brings with it. Bathing in cold water, preferably in a stream or the ocean, is also a very effective way to prepare for magical work or any form of spiritual development.

Active Working

You can also charge water with your own intentions, in much the same way that you charge air in the process of color breathing. Take a glass or other drinking vessel of water, and hold it in front of you with both hands. State your intention in a single sentence, phrase, or word, just as you did in preparation for color breathing, but concentrate on the idea that the intention flows into the water and charges it. Then imagine that the color corresponding most closely to your intention is flowing into the water from all over the universe, coloring the water more and more intensely. Build this imagery as intensely as possible, and then drink the water, concentrating on the idea that you are absorbing the energy you have called into the water.

If you decide to use this method to help you remember your dreams, for example, you might state your intention as "I remember all my dreams," saying these words aloud while holding a glass of water in both hands. Next, imagine blue light flowing toward the glass from every part of the universe, concentrating in the water and turning it bright blue. Hold this image for some time, imagining the water becoming more and more intensely blue, and then drink the water, feeling the blue light flowing into you and improving your ability to remember dreams.

Invoking and Banishing
by the Third Gate

△ This is the third invocation and banishing, and it follows the same pattern as the first two. While it is learned after the work with the Gate of Water, for reasons of balance, it is usually done between air and water, so that you can turn clockwise from east to south to west in the course of the ritual.

Fire in the Druid tradition represents unity and every force and factor that makes diverse things become one. As the third element, it balances air and water, inspiration from without and growth from within, by teaching us that no barrier separates the world outside us from the world inside us. In the unawakened self, it is passion; in the awakened self, it is intentionality. Its symbol is the triangle pointing up, representing the upward movement of flame.

To invoke and banish by fire, turn to the south. With the first two fingers of your right hand trace a triangle with one point up, as shown in the figure, starting at the top point and tracing clockwise. Visualize it in red flame, and then fill it with transparent red flame. Then say words like these: "By the white stag in the light of summer, and in the great name Sul, I invoke the fire, its gods, its spirits, and its powers. May I receive the blessings of fire this day."

Sul is the ancient British goddess of the hot springs at Bath, a goddess of the Sun and also of the fires beneath the earth; her name is pronounced "SUUL," with the Welsh u. If you prefer to work with Irish divinities, Brigid (pronounced "BREEJ"), the goddess of smiths, poets, and healers, is a good choice for this element. Christian Druids invoke Saint Michael the archangel in this quarter.

Once you have finished the invocation, pause for a time, and concentrate on fire. Imagine the hottest day you can remember in the land where you live, and imagine an old dry log catching fire in front of you beneath the hot noonday Sun. Feel the heat from the Sun, the ground, and the flames, and smell the dry air and the tang of wood smoke. As you picture this, feel the powers and blessings of fire flowing into you through your solar plexus. Imagine your body filled with the red light of fire, and feel yourself become so full of flaming energy that nothing could stand against you.

Then say, "I thank the fire for its gifts," and trace the symbol counterclockwise, again from the top of the triangle. Say words like these: "And with the help of the powers of fire, I banish from within me and around me all unbalanced manifestations of fire. I banish them far away from me." Concentrate on the idea that all unbalanced factors in your life are caught up in the flames and burned away until not even the finest ash remains. Take as much time as you need on this visualization.

For the next two or three weeks, include this section in your daily practice: perform the Elemental Cross, then invoke and banish by air, then invoke and banish by fire, then invoke and banish by water, then perform the Circulation of Light. Practice it until you have this phase of the ritual by heart, and can feel fire respond to the ritual. During the time you spend doing this, pay attention to any of the symbols of the Gate of Fire that show up in other aspects of your life. You can also work with the realm of fire by using the following methods.

Receptive Working

Like wind and water, fire forms a reservoir of nwyfre for the Druid mage. In ancient times, according to old legends, Druids would build bonfires of specially chosen magical woods and use the flames to work their magic. In a world where forests need to be preserved and expanded, not sacrificed to human needs, this form of magical working can rarely be justified, but there are other ways to get the same effect.

To make a safe, effective, and ecologically sound magical fire, get a fireproof bowl or small cauldron, preferably of metal. Put it on a heatproof surface in a place where flames and heat can rise for several feet without putting anything at risk. Pour a teaspoon of salt into the bottom of the cauldron. Pour in half a cup or so of pure grain alcohol, or any other alcohol that is at least 150 proof (75 percent alcohol). Light the alcohol with a match, and then sit where you can gaze into the flames. Watch the flames, keeping your attention on them and your mind as clear as possible, until the fire goes out. Allow the energy of the fire to shine into you, and see where it takes you and what unity it brings to you.

Like water, fire absorbs and transforms nwyfre, and you can use it for purification. Set up a magical fire in a place that needs to be purified, light it, and allow the flames to clear away unwanted energies. If you have anything in yourself that needs to be purified or transformed, offer it up to the fire mentally, and gaze into the flames until the fire goes out.

Active Working

The same magical fire can be used in an active way to charge yourself with an intention. Prepare the magical fire as before. As you light the alcohol, say your intention aloud, and then sit where you can gaze into the flames. You can imagine the flames turning an appropriate color as you watch them, but it works as well to simply look into the flames and allow the intention to radiate through its light. Continue gazing into the flames until the last of the fire goes out.

If you want to use this method to strengthen your body's health and vitality, for example, you might choose to state your intention with the phrase "vital force." Prepare the fire bowl, and say aloud the words you chose as you light the alcohol. Sit and gaze into the flames, and be aware of vital force flowing into you in the firelight, until the flames go out.

Invoking and Banishing by the Fourth Gate

This is the fourth invocation and banishing, done after you invoke and banish by air, fire, and water, and it follows the same pattern as the others.

Earth in the Druid tradition is the symbol of manifestation, the firm material basis that allows the other elemental powers to take form in the universe of our experience. In nature, it takes the shape of soil and stone, the substances that make the surface of the Earth; the realm of earth's far depths belongs to Spirit Below instead. The symbol of earth is the creative circle of spirit with a line descending downward into manifestation.

To invoke and banish earth, turn to the north. With the first two fingers of your right hand trace the symbol of earth. In the invoking mode it is traced starting from the place where the circle meets the line and going around the circle clockwise, then drawing the line downward. Visualize it in green flame, and then fill it with paler, transparent green flame. Then say words like the following: "By the great bear who guards the starry heavens, and in the great name Elen, I invoke the earth, its gods, its spirits, and its powers. May I receive the blessings of earth this day."

The goddess Elen appears in Welsh legend as a goddess of dawn and springtime, as well as patroness of the old straight trackways, older than the Romans, that still puzzle wayfarers in the British countryside. In Druid Revival lore she became the goddess of the dragon current flowing along the old tracks, and thus a powerful symbol of life and strength within the Earth. If you prefer to work with Irish deities, Boann, the Irish cow goddess, is a good choice for Earth. Christian Druids usually invoke Saint Uriel the archangel in this quarter.

When you finish the invocation, pause for a time, and concentrate on earth. Imagine the land in which you live, with whatever vegetation flourishes there growing on it. If you live in woodland country, see yourself in the forest; if you live on the plains, imagine yourself on the prairie with tall grasses bending in the wind; if you live in the desert, picture yourself amid the red rock and sagebrush. Be sure to bring in the sounds and scents of the landscape. As you picture this, feel the powers and blessings of earth flowing into you through your solar plexus. Imagine your body filled with the green light of earth, and feel yourself becoming so solid and firm that you could resist the mightiest force in the universe.

Then say, "I thank the earth for its gifts," and trace the symbol in its banishing mode, starting from the place where the circle joins the line, tracing the circle counterclockwise, and then draw the line downward. Say words like the following: "And with the help of the powers of earth, I banish from within me and around me all unbalanced manifestations of earth. I banish them far away from me." Concentrate on the idea that all unbalanced factors in your life are swallowed up by the Earth and buried far beneath soil and stone. Take as much time as you need on this visualization.

For the next two or three weeks, include this section in your daily practice: perform the Elemental Cross, then invoke and banish by air, then invoke and banish by fire, then invoke and banish by water, then invoke and banish by earth, then perform the Circulation of Light. Practice it until you have this phase of the ritual by heart, and can feel the Earth respond to the ritual. During the time you spend doing this, pay attention to any of the symbols of the Gate of Earth that show up in other aspects of your life. You can also work with the realm of earth by using the following methods.

Receptive Working

The living Earth beneath your feet is another reservoir of nwyfre for the Druid mage. Every spot on the Earth's surface has different magical properties, because the soil and stone underlying each place affects the nwyfre that flows up through them. The way a colored filter affects a beam of white light makes a good metaphor for this effect. In some places, the energies that rise up through the land foster human spirituality, and over the centuries, such places have become holy sites and places of pilgrimage. Other places have their own effects, and local folklore often points out places with distinctive powers.

It's useful to arrange a visit to a holy place venerated by traditional lore, or a place that is sacred to you whether or not other people recognize its power, during the time you spend working with the Fourth Gate. When you go there, pause for a time outside the sacred area to clear your mind. Enter the sacred place with the intention of learning from it and experiencing its energies, and keep your mind free of ordinary mental chatter while you're there. If circumstances permit, spend some time meditating while there, taking the place itself as the theme for the meditation. Done in this way, with intention, a visit to a sacred place can be a powerful, transforming experience.

Active Working

You can also charge stones with magical intentions in exactly the same way you charged air and water. Simply choose a stone of a convenient size and shape to carry in your pocket. Wash it with cold water, both to remove dirt and to strip away any unwanted energies that may have become attached to it in the past. Leave it out in direct sunlight for an hour or more to finish the cleansing process. Then pick up the stone and hold it in front of you by the index fingers and thumbs of both hands.

State your intention in a single sentence, phrase, or word, but concentrate on the idea that the intention flows into the stone and charges it. Then imagine that the color corresponding most closely to your intention is flowing into the stone from all over the universe, making the stone glow more and more intensely with that color. Build this imagery as strongly as possible, then release it, and place the stone in your pocket, or in a place where you spend plenty of time.

For example, if you want to improve your skills as a musician, you might define your intention by the phrase "musical skill" and the color green. Choose and clean a pebble that suits your fancy, and charge it as described above. Put the pebble in the room where you practice music most often, close to the place where you sit or stand while playing.

Invoking by the Fifth Gate

This is the fifth invocation, done after you invoke and banish by air, fire, water, and earth, but no banishing is done with any of the three forms of spirit. Banishing belongs purely to the realms of the four material elements, since in the realms of spirit nothing needs banishing.

Spirit Below represents the deep places of the Earth. The world that human beings inhabit consists of four overlapping spheres, one each of fire, air, water, and earth—the upper atmosphere corresponding to fire; the lower atmosphere to air; the seas, rivers, lakes, and groundwater to water; and the solid crust of the planet, to earth. Below that lies a realm as alien to human life as the furthest reaches of outer space, a realm of unimaginable heat, pressure, and energy that drives the continents across the face of the planet and sets the land trembling with earthquakes. This is the realm of Spirit Below. Its symbol is the plain circle of Spirit.

To invoke Spirit Below, face the same direction you faced during the Elemental Cross. Trace a clockwise circle below and in front of you, as though tracing it over an altar. Visualize your fingers drawing the circle in orange flame, and fill it with paler, transparent orange flame. Then say words like these: "By the bright heart of the Earth Mother, and in the great name Ced, I invoke Spirit Below, its gods, its spirits, and its powers. May I receive the blessings of Spirit Below this day."

In Welsh Druid lore, Ced is the goddess of living nature and the source of all life. Her name is pronounced "KEHD," and means "bounty" or "help" in Welsh. If you prefer to work with Irish divinities, the goddess Danu, mother of all the gods and goddesses, is a good choice for this element. Christian Druids often invoke the Virgin Mary at this Station.

When you finish the invocation, pause for a time, and concentrate on Spirit Below. Picture in your mind's eye the ground beneath your feet, the soil and stone that belongs to the element of earth, and then go deeper, into the heart of the living planet itself. Feel the immense power that drives earthquakes and volcanoes, lifts mountains toward the sky, and moves entire continents across the face of the planet, and sense that same power surging through every living thing from the smallest microbe to the great whales and the tallest trees.

As you picture all this, feel the powers and blessings of Spirit Below flowing into you through your solar plexus. Imagine the rich harvest orange light of spirit below filling your body, and feel the life force of the planet leaping through your veins. Take as much time as seems appropriate for this visualization. Then say, "I thank Spirit Below for its gifts."

For the next two or three weeks, include this section in your daily practice. Perform the Elemental Cross, then invoke and banish by air, fire, water, and earth, then invoke Spirit Below, and then perform the Circulation of Light. Practice it until you have this phase of the ritual by heart, and can feel Spirit Below respond to the ritual. During the time you spend doing this, pay attention to any symbols of the Gate of Spirit Below that show up in other aspects of your life. You can also work with the realm of Spirit Below by using the following methods.

Receptive Working

The deep places of the Earth are the home of the telluric current, one of the two primary currents of nwyfre used in Druid magic. The telluric current flows through the crust and takes on the qualities of stones and metals as it flows through them. It can be contacted anywhere in the realms of the four elements.

A useful way to draw on the telluric current is the receptive working for Spirit Below, the Telluric Nwyfre exercise. It should be done in a place where you can stand on bare ground, grass, or some other natural surface.

Stand with your feet shoulder-width apart with your elbows out a few inches from your sides, your forearms and hands parallel to the ground, wrists straight, palms facing down and fingers pointing forward, as though you were resting your hands and forearms on a flat surface to either side of you. Relax your arms as much as possible and spread your fingers gently apart. Try to feel the presence of the Earth beneath you; with practice, you'll begin to sense a current of energy flowing up from below. Breathe slowly and deeply for one to three minutes, feeling energy flowing into your fingertips.

Then bring them inward toward the vital center an inch below your navel, stopping a few inches from your body, palms toward you and fingertips nearly touching. Imagine the Earth currents flowing from your fingertips into the midline of your body. After a short time, move your hands slowly upward, maintaining the imagery, pouring the telluric current into the midline of your body from the vital center up to the throat center. At this point separate your hands, sweeping them up and out to your sides, and bow deeply, then return to the first position with hands turned toward the earth. Three or nine cycles of the exercise are enough.

Active Working

The active working for Spirit Below belongs to a more advanced level of practice and is covered in a later section of this book.

Invoking by the Sixth Gate

This is the sixth invocation, done after you invoke and banish by air, fire, water, and earth, and invoke Spirit Below. Spirit Above represents the universe beyond the limits of the

Earth. Just as the world we inhabit, with its four elemental spheres, stops a few miles below our feet where the Earth's crust gives way to the mantle, it stops a few miles above our heads at the borders of space. Beyond these are the vast reaches where stars and planets circle through the void. This realm shares the same symbol as Spirit Below, the plain circle of spirit.

To invoke Spirit Above, turn to face the same direction you faced during the Elemental Cross. Trace a clockwise circle above you, visualizing it in violet flame. Fill it with paler, transparent violet flame. Then say words like these: "By the Sun in its glory, the father of light, and in the great name Celi, I invoke Spirit Above, its gods, its spirits, and its powers. May I receive the blessings of Spirit Above this day."

In Welsh Druid traditions, Celi is the hidden god of the heavens, the original source of the three rays of light that brought the worlds into being. His name is pronounced "KEH-lee." If you prefer to work with Irish gods and goddesses, the Dagda is a good choice for this element; his name, pronounced "DOY-da," means "the excellent god," and he is the father of the Irish gods. Christian Druids usually invoke Christ in this Station.

When you have finished the invocation, pause for a time, and concentrate on Spirit Above. Picture in your mind's eye the Sun at midheaven above you, surrounded by the planets in their orbits, with numberless stars scattered across the infinite heavens beyond. Sense the vastness of space, the cold pure starlight that fills it, and the perfect order that governs all the worlds in their courses.

As you picture all this, feel the powers and blessings of Spirit Above flowing into you. Imagine the intense purple light of Spirit Above filling your body through your solar plexus, and feel your awareness opening outward so that, for a moment, you seem to understand the whole cosmos. Take as much time as seems appropriate for this visualization. Then say, "I thank Spirit Above for its gifts."

For the next two or three weeks, include this section in your daily practice: perform the Elemental Cross, then invoke and banish by air, fire, water, and earth, then invoke Spirit Below and Spirit Above, and then perform the Circulation of Light. Practice it until you have this phase of the ritual by heart, and can feel Spirit Above respond to the ritual. During the time you spend doing this, pay attention to any of the symbols of the Gate of Spirit Above that show up in other aspects of your life. You can also work with the realm of Spirit Above by using the following methods.

Receptive Working

The heavens are a potent reservoir of power for magic, and every star and planet has its own magical energy that can be experienced and used. The most powerful and positive force in the skies of our Earth, though, is the Sun, the source of light and life for our world, and your work with Spirit Above should focus on the Sun's energy to begin with. Later, as you gain experience, you can study other branches of this lore.

A useful way to draw on Spirit Above through the light and nwyfre of the Sun is the Solar Nwyfre Exercise. This should be done in the morning, between dawn and 10:00 AM, when the skies are clear. Find a place outside where you can stand in the Sun's rays, wearing as little clothing as possible. Stand facing the Sun, your feet shoulder-width apart, your eyes closed, with as much of your body as possible in sunlight. Raise your arms out to the sides so that your arms extend to the sides in the form of a cross, your fingertips point out to the sides and your palms are turned to face the Sun. Relax your arms and gently spread your fingers. Breathe slowly, concentrating on feeling the sunlight soaking into your body, especially into your fingertips.

After one to three minutes, move both hands inwards to your head, stopping a few inches from your forehead, palms facing you, fingers nearly touching each other. Imagine the sunlight flowing from the fingertips into the middle of your head. Next, move your hands slowly down from forehead to solar plexus, maintaining the imagery, pouring light from your fingertips into the midline of your body. When your hands reach solar plexus level, sweep them out to the sides and bow as low as you can, then return to the first position with your arms spread wide to greet the Sun. Repeat the entire process three or nine times.

Active Method

As with Spirit Below, the active method of working with spirit above belongs to a more advanced level of practice and is studied in detail later in this book.

Invoking by the Seventh Gate

This is the final invocation of the Sphere of Protection, done after you invoke and banish by air, fire, water, and earth, and invoke Spirit Above and Below. Spirit Within, in the Druid tradition, represents the presence of life and spirit within everything in the world, including you and me. Where some religions see human beings as something set apart from the rest of the world and equally far from the divine, Druidry recognizes that human beings are part of one great reality, along with stones, trees, gods, and everything else there is.

For this reason, the symbol of Spirit Within is nothing other than yourself.

To invoke Spirit Within, remain facing the same direction you faced during the Elemental Cross, and be aware of the six powers you have already invoked—air in the east, fire in the south, water in the west, earth in the north, Spirit Below in the land beneath you and Spirit Above in the heavens above. See yourself in the midst of these six powers, in the place of perfect balance among them. Then say words like the following: "By the six powers here invoked and here present, and in the grand word Awen, I invoke Spirit Within. May the universe within me and the universe around me be in harmony."

The word *Awen* is not the name of a god. Rather, it is the great keyword of the Druid Revival, an archaic Welsh word meaning "spirit of inspiration." Through Awen the worlds came into existence at the beginning of time; through Awen poets, artists, and all other creative people receive their talents; through Awen, magic becomes the art of participation in the great powers of the cosmos. In Druidry it is pronounced in three parts, drawn out like "Aaaaa-ooooo-ennnnn." The first part, the sound of the Ogham few Ailm, stands for the sky and the solar current; the second, the sound of Ur, stands for the Earth and the telluric current; the third, the sound of Nuin, stands for the individual human being as the connecting link between them.

When you finish the invocation, pause for a time, and concentrate on Spirit Within. Be aware of yourself exactly as you are, and strive to see every aspect of yourself as a vessel of infinite powers. Imagine yourself filled with the pure white light of Spirit Within, and feel yourself in harmony with the whole cosmos. Take as much time as seems appropriate for this visualization. Then say "I thank Spirit Within for its gifts." At this point, focus on the center of energies at your heart, and proceed at once to the Circulation of Light.

Once you have learned to invoke by all the Seven Gates and banish by the Gates of the elements, you have learned the entire Sphere of Protection ritual. Plan on practicing it once each day for as long as you follow the path of Druid magic. You can also work with the realm of Spirit Within by using the following methods.

Receptive Working

Trees and other green growing things form one of the classic Druid emblems of Spirit Within. The reasons are complex, touching on the deep reaches of magical philosophy and practice, but one explanation deserves discussion here. Human beings and trees exchange energy easily and benefit each other in the process. Just as trees thrive on carbon dioxide, which human beings breathe out as a waste product, and produce oxygen that human beings need to survive, so the energy given off by many trees heals humans, while energy from humans nurtures trees. The same is true of other plants, and indeed many other things in the natural world, and an entire system of Druid natural medicine unfolds from the same principle.

Start the exercise by selecting a tree. Some varieties are considered more beneficial to human beings than others: pine, fir, and cedar are held to be best, with oak, beech, and apple not far behind. Elm is traditionally avoided, as its energies are unhealthy for human beings.

You'll need to ask the tree's permission before exchanging energy with it. Like other nonhuman creatures, trees don't understand human language, but they do understand our emotional patterns—often better than we do. Stand before the tree, and ask it silently if it's willing to share its nwyfre with you. Feel for the answer and behave accordingly.

If the tree gives permission, approach it, and come in contact with it. There are two traditional ways to do this. The first focuses the healing effects on your nervous system. To do this, stand or sit with your back pressed against the trunk. You can amplify the effect by putting your left hand on the small of your back with the palm turned out, touching the tree, and your right hand on your belly just below the navel, palm in.

The second focuses the healing effects on the organs of your chest and abdomen. To do this, face the tree with your feet a few inches away from the base of the trunk, then lean the front of your body and your forehead against the tree. You can heighten the effect by placing your hands at forehead level, forming an upward-pointing triangle with your thumbs and index fingers, spreading the other fingers comfortably. Let your forehead rest in the center of the triangle. Your arms bend around the trunk, as though embracing the tree with your elbows.

In either posture, relax your body as much as possible, and feel the tree as a living presence. An attitude of openness, friendship, and affection will yield the best results here. Ten or fifteen minutes of quiet presence next to a large, healthy tree will leave your own nwyfre cleansed and energized, and will do much the same thing for the tree.

Active Working

As with Spirit Above and Below, the active working for Spirit Within belongs to a more advanced level of magical work and is discussed later in this book.

CHAPTER 5
The Grove of the Druids

The Sphere of Protection ritual forms the foundation of the system of Druid magic taught in this book. Once you can do all the phases of that ritual from memory, many other dimensions of ritual work can be added to it. The first step in this direction is the use of the Sphere of Protection itself as a basic ritual for practical magic. One of the advantages of the Sphere is that this takes nothing more than a change in the words and intentions in the Calling of the Elements.

Before you take this step, however, you may want to take another look at the material on magic, intentionality, and ethics in the first chapter of this book. Like any other form of power, magic can be misused and mishandled, and it can also blow up in your face. Since the magical movements of nwyfre follow your intentionality, the best way to get good results is to be sure your intentionality will create a world you can live with over the long term.

Several useful guidelines can help you do this more effectively. First, before you perform a working, be careful in choosing the goal you hope to achieve. You should be able to express it clearly in a word, a phrase, or at most a single short sentence, without the least bit of ambiguity. Like the man in the joke who told the genie, "Make me a milkshake," and got turned into a milkshake, those who express their intentions in magic sloppily often get results they neither want nor expect.

When choosing an intention for magic, it is important to be sure that what you intend is actually what you want. It is equally important to aim for your goal, not for something you think will get you to your goal. Plenty of people who have no idea they practice magic fall into the trap of pursuing means rather than ends, and get what they ask for but not what they actually want. If you want self-respect but your intention focuses on money, or you want love but your intention focuses on getting a particular person's sexual favors, or you want a meaningful life but your intention focuses on success symbols, you're going to be disappointed, because you'll get the thing you ask for rather than the thing you really want.

For this reason, before you perform a magical working, it's wise to meditate on it at least three times. Use your intention as the theme for these meditations. As you explore it, think about what your intention will mean to you when you achieve it. Turn a cold eye on your fantasies, whatever those happen to be, and seek a sense of the real effects of the change you want in your life. If you end up deciding that your intention isn't what you want, scrap it and work out something better.

Another essential step is casting a divination before you perform any working. Your question should be along the lines of, "What do I most need to understand about the magical working I am considering?" The simple three-few reading given in chapter 3 (Figure 3-3) can be used for this purpose, with the first few standing for the situation, the second for the working you have in mind, and the third for the results. Pay careful attention to the results you get, and let yourself be guided by it. If you get an unfavorable reading, don't ignore it and go blindly ahead anyway!

Once you have done these preliminary steps, proceed to the magical work. Two examples show how this kind of work can be done. Experiment with both of them, and then work out your own variations on the Sphere of Protection ritual.

Transforming Yourself

One of the classic applications of the Sphere ritual focuses on making changes in yourself by invoking desired qualities and banishing unwanted ones. You can do this in a general way, invoking four qualities and banishing four others, or you can do it in a more tightly focused way, invoking a single quality and banishing its opposite.

How does this work? If you're using the general approach, start by choosing one quality you want to develop in yourself, and one quality you wish you had less of, for each of the four material elements. For example, you might decide that as a mage in training, you need more of air's quickness of mind, fire's strength of will, water's desire to learn, and earth's patience. You might equally decide that you need less of air's wandering thoughts, fire's irritability, water's depressed moods, and earth's laziness. You would explore these concepts in meditation, decide that the changes you have named are right for you, and then perform a divination to make sure your intention is in tune with the cosmos.

When you perform your Sphere of Protection each day, then, invoke the quality you want to increase in yourself while working with each element, and banish the quality you want to decrease. For example, when you go to the east and trace the symbol of air, you might say words like these: "By the hawk of May in the heights of heaven, and in the great name Hu, I invoke the air, its gods, its spirits and its powers. May the powers of air bless me with quickness of mind." Imagine the yellow nwyfre of air sweeping into you, setting your mind into swift and nimble motion. Then thank the powers of air, trace the air symbol counterclockwise, and say words like these: "And with the help of the powers of air, I banish from within and around me all wandering thoughts. I banish them far away from me." Pause, and imagine that your mind's habit of wandering is swept away by the winds and loses itself in the vastness of air.

Do the same thing to the south, west, and north, invoking and banishing the qualities of the other elements. When you complete the circle, invoke Spirit Below, concentrate on all of the changes you want to make in yourself. As you trace the circle of Spirit, say words like these: "By the bright heart of the Earth Mother, and in the great name Ced, I invoke Spirit Below, its gods, its spirits, and its powers. May the powers of Spirit Below strengthen quickness of mind, strength of will, desire to learn, and patience in me, and may they assist me to release wandering thoughts, irritability, depressed moods, and laziness from myself and my life." Concentrate on the orange nwyfre of Spirit Below flowing into you from above and feel the changes you have willed taking place in you, and then thank Spirit Below in your own words. Do the same thing, changing the words and colored nwyfre as needed, for Spirit Above and Spirit Within, and close with the Circulation of Light as usual.

If you want to use the more focused approach, simply adapt the general approach by invoking the same quality in each of the directions, and banishing its opposite. For example, if you find that old fears from childhood are hindering your life more than anything else, you might choose to invoke courage and banish fear in each of the four directions, and call on the three forms of Spirit to seal the transformation.

Before using either approach, meditation is an essential preparation, and not only because you want to be careful before invoking changes in yourself. The more clearly you understand the changes you have in mind, the stronger and more exact your intention will be and the better the results of the ritual. This is especially important with the more focused approach, since you need to understand how the quality you invoke relates to each of the four material elements.

If you choose the second example, for instance, you will find that each element has its own mode of courage. Air brings the courage of clarity that shrinks fears down to size; fire brings the courage of will that overwhelms all resistance; water brings the courage of joy that laughs in the face of danger; earth brings the courage of persistence that moves steadily ahead despite all opposition. Each mode of courage also has its corresponding mode of fear. The better you understand these details, and the more you bring that understanding into the ritual, the better the results will be.

Another important magical principle comes into play once you finish the ritual. As soon as possible after you finish the working, take some practical step toward the fulfillment of your intention. The action you choose can be very small. For example, if you do the focused working to bring courage and banish fear, choose something that frightens you just a little, and do it. Pay attention to your emotional reactions to the thing you choose, but do it anyway. This grounds the effects of the working in your ordinary surroundings and helps the patterns you have established in nwyfre affect the material world.

Whether you choose the more general or the more focused approach, perform the Sphere of Protection ritual with the same focus at least seven times, and keep track of the results in your Druid journal. This is a potent technique and you may be surprised by how quickly the results start showing up in your life.

Transforming the World

The same approach can also be used to bring about changes in the world around you. This requires greater care, since the ethical issues are usually more intense, and it also requires more effort, since changing things outside yourself means you have to shape the flow of much larger patterns of nwyfre. For both these reasons, among others, it's wise to meditate thoroughly on any such project before you attempt it. It also helps to try for fairly modest results at first, and work up to larger projects once you get experience with the method.

The method is exactly the same as the more focused method for personal transformation just given. As with any other magical working, you need to choose your intention carefully, so you can state it in a single word, phrase, or short sentence. When you complete the Elemental Cross and go to the east to invoke air, change the wording of the invocation to ask the powers of air to accomplish your intention, stating it aloud. When you banish, banish every influence that might hinder your intention. Do the same thing in the other three quarters. When you return to the center, invoke Spirit in its three forms to confirm the accomplishment of your intention.

For example, if you need access to an old book of Druid lore that is out of print and unavailable to you, you would start by meditating on that intention several times, making sure your intention is ethical and that you can ask for exactly what you want. You might end up stating your intention as "A copy of Ross Nichols' book *The Cosmic Shape* comes to me." You would then cast a divination to be sure the working is a good idea. If so, in your next Sphere of Protection working, when you invoke the element of air, you would use words such as these: "By the hawk of May in the heights of morning, and in the great name Hu, I invoke the air, its gods, its spirits, and its powers. With the help of the powers of air, a copy of Ross Nichols' book *The Cosmic Shape* comes to me."

You would then imagine the book coming to you, brought by the winds and the spirits of the air, and then thank the air in your own words. As you trace the banishing version of the symbol of air, say words such as these: "And with the help of the powers of air, I banish every influence that might hinder my intention. I banish it far away from me." Imagine that every obstacle that keeps you from getting the book dissolves like mist. Proceed to the south and around the circle as usual, repeating words of the same type in each quarter, changing them to suit the element of that quarter.

When you complete the circle and invoke Spirit Below, trace the circle of Spirit and say words such as these: "By the bright heart of the Earth Mother, and in the great name Ced, I invoke Spirit Below, its gods, its spirits and its powers. May the powers of Spirit Below guide the elements in their work, so that a copy of Ross Nichols' book *The Cosmic Shape* comes to me." As you say this, imagine the book resting in your hands. See it in your mind's eye as clearly as possible; imagine the weight of the book, the texture of its paper dust jacket, the scent of old book paper.

Concentrate on the image of the book resting in your hands; let go of everything else for the moment. Remember, you're not trying to force the universe to do what you want; you're simply formulating a pattern into which currents of nwyfre will flow. When you are ready, release the image entirely and go on with the ritual. Do the same thing when you invoke Spirit Above and Spirit Within. When you do the Circulation of Light, imagine that the spinning spheres of light set the world into motion around you, sending your intention out to the edges of the universe. Once again, after you finish the ritual, take some practical step toward bringing about your intention—to continue the example, you might go onto the Internet and do a book search for *The Cosmic Shape*. Keep track of the results in your Druid journal.

The Grove Ceremony

The Sphere of Protection is a complete ritual in its own right, but it also forms one part of a more extensive ritual, the grove ceremony. This ceremony is the key to the more advanced dimensions of this book's magical work, and should be studied, practiced, and mastered as soon as you can do the Sphere of Protection effectively from memory.

In eighteenth- and nineteenth-century Druidry, a grove was a local group of Druids who held regular meetings with ritual openings and closings. *Grove,* in Druid parlance, in other words, meant much the same thing that *lodge* means among Freemasons. It still has this meaning, but during the development of Druid magic in the twentieth century, Druids of several traditions realized that the same ritual used to open and close a grove could also be done by a Druid working alone, as a way of opening and closing magical ceremonies.

Used in this way, these rituals perform the essential tasks of establishing magical space and time at the beginning of a working, and returning the mage to ordinary space and time at the working's end.

Grove ceremonies from many different Druid traditions can be used for this purpose—I have used half a dozen from time to time with good effect—but most traditions keep their grove rituals private and only communicate them to initiates. The Ancient Order of Druids in America (AODA), by contrast, makes the complete text of its grove ritual public. For this reason among others, the AODA grove opening and closing is used here. Still, if you are an initiate of another Druid order and like to use its grove ritual as a solitary practice, you can use all the magical methods in this book within the framework of that ritual, too.

Opening the Grove

Before you start the opening ritual, you need to gather everything required and put it in its proper place. The requirements for the grove ritual, and for the workings that will take place in an open grove, are fairly simple. You'll need something to serve as an altar—a small end table or folding TV tray will do fine—a white altar cloth, and a chair suitable for meditation.

You'll also need four bowls or small cauldrons. They will all need to fit on top of the altar at the same time, and leave room for other ritual needs and equipment, so "small" is the operative word. Two of them will be filled halfway with dry sand; one of these will be used for incense, and the other for a votive candle or tea light. The third will be half-full of water, and the last one will be half-full of salt or clean earth. They represent the four material elements and play an important role in the ritual.

Finally, you'll need to decide what you want to do about garments. A plain white robe and *nemyss*—this latter is a vaguely Egyptian headcloth that is tied around the head and falls down over the shoulders, as shown in Figure 5-1—has long been standard ritual wear in the Druid Revival tradition, but it's also a central theme in modern Druidry that each Druid has the right to make his or her own choices. Some Druid mages wear the classic white robe and nemyss; others wear some other sort of ritual garments; still others do magic in their street clothes or wearing nothing at all. Make your own decision depending on your circumstances and preferences.

To prepare the space, set up the altar in the center, put the altar cloth over it, and put the cauldron of incense on it toward the east side. The cauldron of fire goes to the south, the cauldron of water to the west, and the cauldron of salt to

Figure 5-1   A Druid Nemyss

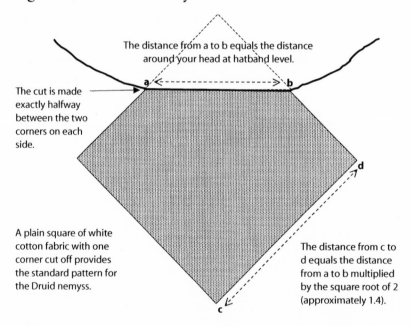

The distance from a to b equals the distance around your head at hatband level.

The cut is made exactly halfway between the two corners on each side.

A plain square of white cotton fabric with one corner cut off provides the standard pattern for the Druid nemyss.

The distance from c to d equals the distance from a to b multiplied by the square root of 2 (approximately 1.4).

the north, as shown in Figure 5-2. The chair goes to the north, facing south toward the altar, with enough space between them so that you can pass through readily. When you've learned the grove ritual and are using it for magical workings, any additional tools or materials go on the altar as well. Just before you begin, put a stick or cone of incense in the incense cauldron and light it, and light the candle or tea lamp in the cauldron of fire. That completes the preparation of the space.

Before you begin, take a few moments to clear your mind of unrelated thoughts and feelings. Then, when you are ready to begin, enter the circle and walk in a clockwise circle to the north side of the altar, between the altar and the chair, where you face south. Raise your right hand palm forward to salute the Sun, which is always symbolically at high noon in the southern sky. Visualize it there, shining down its rays of power and blessing on you and the entire world.

Say aloud, "Let the powers be present as I am about to open a grove of Druids in this place. The first duty of a Druid in the Sacred Grove is to proclaim peace to the four quarters of the world, for without peace my work cannot proceed."

Figure 5-2 The Druid Altar

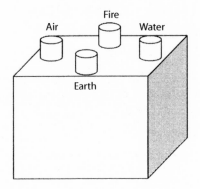

Circle around to the east. Face outward and raise your right hand palm outward to salute the direction. Say, "I proclaim peace in the east." As you do this, imagine peace enfolding the whole quarter of the world to the east of you. At the same time, be aware of your mind and thoughts, and still them, so that peace is present in the symbolic east of yourself.

Proceed to the south and make the same gesture, saying, "I proclaim peace in the south." Imagine peace spreading across the southern quarter of the world. At the same time, be aware of your passions and desires, and still them, establishing peace in the symbolic south of yourself.

Proceed to the west, and do the same thing, saying, "I proclaim peace in the west." Imagine peace spreading over the western quarter of the world. At the same time, be aware of your feelings and emotions, and still them, making peace in the symbolic west of yourself.

Proceed to the north and do the same thing, saying, "I proclaim peace in the north." Imagine peace spreading across the northern quarter of the world. At the same time, be aware of your physical senses, and still them, so that peace comes to the symbolic north of yourself.

Return to the north side of the altar, facing south as you were at the beginning of the ritual, and say, "The four quarters are at peace and the work of the grove may proceed. Let this grove and all within it be purified with air."

Go to the eastern side of the altar, pick up the cauldron with the incense in both hands. Imagine that it is surrounded with a sphere of brilliant yellow light. Carry it to the eastern edge of the space. Walk in a clockwise circle once around the outer edge of the space, from east to east, and as you do, imagine the sphere of yellow light tracing a luminous circle that surrounds and protects the entire grove. Feel the winds of heaven rushing around the circle as you go. When you come back around to the east, return the cauldron to the altar.

Next, say, "Let this grove and all within it be purified with fire." Pick up the cauldron with the lamp, imagining that it is surrounded by a sphere of brilliant red light. Take it to the southern edge of the space and go once around clockwise from south to south, tracing a circle of red light that surrounds and protects the grove. Imagine that flames rise and sweep around the circle as you go. When you've come back around to the south, return the cauldron to the altar.

Next, say, "Let this grove and all within it be purified with water." Pick up the cauldron with the water, imagining that it is surrounded with a sphere of brilliant blue light. Take it to the western edge of the space and go once around clockwise from west to west, tracing a circle of blue light that surrounds and protects the grove. Imagine that waves of water rush around the circle as you go. When you've come back around to the west, return the cauldron to the altar.

Next, say, "Let this grove and all within it be purified with earth." Pick up the cauldron with the salt or earth, imagining that it is surrounded with a sphere of brilliant green light. Take it to the northern edge of the space and go once around clockwise from north to north, tracing a circle of green light that surrounds and protects the grove. Imagine that a grove of mighty trees springs up around the circle as you go. When you've come back around to the north, return the cauldron to the altar.

Standing at the north of the altar, facing south, say, "I invoke the blessing of the Mighty Ones with the words that have been the bond among all Druids:

Grant, O holy ones, thy protection;
And in protection, strength;
And in strength, understanding;
And in understanding, knowledge;
And in knowledge, the knowledge of justice;
And in the knowledge of justice, the love of it;
And in that love, the love of all existences;
And in the love of all existences, the love of Earth our
    mother and all goodness.

When you've finished the prayer, chant the word *Awen* three times. Draw the word out into its three syllables— "Ah-Oh-En"—and let it resonate throughout your body and the grove.

Pause for a moment, then perform the complete Sphere of Protection ritual. In each of the seven invocations, ask the powers of the elements to bless and protect the grove, and in each of the banishings, banish any influence that might hinder the grove and its work. In the east, for example, you might invoke with words like these: "By the hawk of May in the heights of morning, and in the great name Hu, I invoke the air, its gods, its spirits, and its powers. May the powers of air bless and protect this grove and all within it, and grant their aid its work." You might banish with words like these: "And with the help of the powers of air, I banish from within and around this grove every influence that might hinder its work. I banish all such influences far away." When you do the Circulation of Light, finally, expand the whirling sphere of light far enough that it surrounds the entire working space.

When you are finished doing the Sphere of Protection, go to the chair and sit down. This act completes the opening half of the ceremony.

Closing the Grove

When the work of the grove is finished, return to the chair, sit down, and let your mind return to stillness. When you're ready, rise and go to the north side of the altar, facing south across it as at the beginning. Say, "Let the powers be present as I am about to close a grove of Druids in this place. Peace prevails in the four quarters and throughout the grove. Let any power remaining from this working be returned to the Earth for its blessing."

This is a crucial step, and takes practice. Any magical working leaves some nwyfre behind it, and this needs to be earthed out so it doesn't affect others or manifest in your life in unwanted ways. Feel the energy of the working around you, and then imagine it flowing inward toward the altar, down through it into the Earth, and then down to the Earth's center. Keep concentrating on this until the ritual space feels clear of any leftover nwyfre.

Next, say, "I now invoke the Sword of Swords." Pause, and imagine that a great sword rises through the altar, hilt first, as though through the surface of a lake. The blade is of blue steel that shimmers with a light like Sun on water, the hilt is of brilliant gold, and the pommel at the upper end of the hilt is a jewel that shimmers and flashes in rainbow colors. The sword rises until it has cleared the altar and hovers in the air, its point just above the altar's surface. Repeat the following invocation of the Sword of Swords:

> From the rising Sun, three rays of light;
> From the living earth, three stones of witness;
> From the eye and mind and hand of wisdom,
> Three rowan staves of all knowledge.
> From the fire of the Sun, the forge;

From the bones of the earth, the steel;
From the hand of the wise, the shaping:
From these, Excalibur.

Raise your right hand in salute, and imagine yourself placing your palm against the flat of the blade, as knights once did when swearing fealty. Say, "By the Sword of Swords, I pledge my faithful service to the living Earth our home and mother. Awen."

Chant the word *Awen* in three syllables, "Ah-Oh-En," drawing each one out. As you do, see the image of the sword dissolve into brilliant light and disappear. You are left standing before the altar, your hand raised in salute to the Sun in the south. Lower your hand, leave the altar, walk in a clockwise circle around the space, and then continue around to the exit and leave the grove. This completes the closing half of the ceremony.

Working Magic in the Grove

What you can do between the opening and closing halves of the grove ceremony is limited only by your imagination and your understanding of magic. To begin with, practice the two halves of the ceremony until you can do both from memory. Until you can get by without a written copy of the ceremony, its deeper dimensions are out of reach, and taking the step to serious magical practice should be postponed.

Once you can do the grove opening and closing smoothly from memory, you can begin working magic within the sacred space established by the grove ceremony. The magical techniques you've already learned provide the basic toolkit for this work.

First Method

To begin with, the method for doing practical work with the Sphere of Protection ritual gains a good deal of magical force when done in an open grove. Simply change the invocations and banishings of the Sphere ritual in the opening ceremony as needed to suit your intention. This is a simple but complete form of ritual working, and, with practice, it can easily have effects as potent as much more complex ceremonies.

For example, if your intention is to use magic to develop your abilities as an artist, you would do the usual preliminaries of meditating on the intention and casting an Ogham reading to be sure the working is appropriate. You might then begin with the grove opening, proclaiming peace to the four quarters, purifying the grove with the four material elements, and invoking the gods with the Druid Prayer, and beginning the Sphere of Protection with your usual Elemental Cross. When you invoke in the east, though, use words that call on the powers of air to help you develop your artistic abilities, and when you banish, banish all obstacles to the free expression of your artistic vision.

Proceed to the other six elements and express your intention in the same way. Do the Circulation of Light as usual, and then take your seat in the grove. Spend several minutes concentrating on your intention, not as something you want to achieve in your future, but as though you have it at that moment; feel creative power flowing through you, trembling at your fingertips, demanding to be expressed. Begin the closing ritual while this feeling is still strong in you, and close in the usual way. As soon as possible after finishing, take some practical step toward the fulfillment of your intention—for example, you might get out your art supplies and start work on a new drawing, painting, or sculpture.

Second Method

When you have done several workings of this sort and know your way around the method, the next step is to integrate the simple magical workings introduced in chapter 4. The active workings for air, water, fire, and earth can all be used in this way. Start with anything you need—a glass of water, the material for a magical fire, or a stone—at the center of the altar. Perform the opening half of the grove ritual as usual, putting your intention into the invocations and banishings of the Sphere of Protection ritual, as in the first method described.

Take your seat in the grove and concentrate on your intention. Imagine the nwyfre charged with your intention as colored light filling the grove, using the color symbolism that was presented in Table 4-1. At this point, go on to the active working you have chosen: breathe the color into your body, concentrate it in the water or the stone, or light the magical fire and gaze into the flames. When you have finished, spend some time concentrating on your intention as something completed, and then proceed to the closing half of the ceremony.

If you decide to use this second method with the same intention as the first, for example, after meditating on your intention and casting an Ogham reading to be sure the working is appropriate, you would make the usual preparations for a grove ritual, and you might place a glass or goblet half-full of pure water in the middle of the altar. You would open in the same way, and use similar words in the Sphere of Protection.

As you finish opening the grove, though, you might imagine the nwyfre summoned by the Sphere of Protection as purple light filling the entire space. Take your seat in the grove, and pay attention to the nwyfre you have summoned, then imagine it moving inward to the center of the grove and flowing into the water. Using your imagination, press the purple light inward, into the water, until it has been completely absorbed and the water is practically fizzing with nwyfre. Rise and take up the glass in both hands, clear your mind completely, and then drink the water.

Return to your seat in the grove, sit down, and spend some time concentrating on your intention, not as something you hope to achieve but as though you have already achieved it. When you are ready, begin the closing half of the grove ceremony, and close in the usual way. As before, take some practical step toward the fulfillment of your intention as soon as possible after you finish the working.

The Art of Scrying

Another use for the grove ceremony is as a starting point for inner journeys, using the imagination as a gateway. Distrust and fear of imagination is so deeply rooted in modern culture that many people dismiss such journeys as empty make-believe, and others who reject this prejudice react by putting too much emphasis on imaginative experience. These two extremes define a binary, of course, and the third factor defines an important branch of magical work.

The word *scrying* is an old term for "seeing," and still gets some play in modern English in the form *descry,* meaning "to see at a distance." In magical circles, though, it long ago turned into a word for a kind of seeing that does not rely on the physical eyes. Like so many magical techniques, scrying is something everyone does all the time without noticing it. Mages simply noticed this, learned to do it consciously, and put it to work.

Scrying, in fact, is nothing more than the art of seeing with the imagination. Take a few moments right now to imagine something—a weathered gray standing stone, let's say, with grass around its base and patches of white lichen growing on it here and there. You don't have to "see it" as though it's physically in front of you. Simply let the image rise in your mind's eye, and see what your imagination adds to it. As you look at the stone, what lies beyond it? What is the weather and the time of day? Is the wind blowing, and if so, from what direction? Don't try to reason these questions out, or force the image to go one way or another; simply let your imagination play, and see what it shows you.

If you took the time to do that just now, you have just had your first scrying experience. It really is that simple! Mages usually practice scrying in a ritual or meditative setting, however, in order to focus the inner eye of scrying more intently on a chosen subject. The grove ceremony offers an effective framework for doing this, and seven imaginal spaces—the realms beyond the Seven Gates—as destinations for your first imaginal journeys.

Start by setting up the grove in the usual way, except that the chair is placed so that it faces across the altar toward the direction of the element you intend to scry—for example, the chair will be in the west facing east to scry air, and in the south facing north to scry fire. (Leave it in the north to scry the three forms of Spirit.) Open the grove as usual, with the standard grove ceremony version of the Sphere of Protection. Take your seat, and go through the same process you would use to begin a meditation: relaxation, followed by the cleansing breath, followed by five minutes or so of rhythmic breathing. Do this as color breathing, using the color of the gate you plan to enter, to begin attuning yourself to its energies.

When you have finished the period of rhythmic breath, imagine that a circle of great trees surrounds the grove. Just within the circle of trees, the symbols of the elements hover in the air, brightly colored. Beneath you is the rich warm earth of the forest floor, marked with the orange circle of Spirit Below, and the sky and the purple circle of Spirit Above are overhead. Hear the wind in the branches and the calls of birds, and smell the scent of leaves and earth and fresh forest air. This is the Inner Grove, your sanctuary and place of Druid magic in the imaginal world. You will be returning to it at the beginning and end of each of your imaginal journeys, so take the time to imagine it richly and strongly.

Then imagine yourself rising to your feet and going to the center of the Inner Grove. Face the symbol of whichever element you have chosen to scry. Imagine it expanding until it is large enough for you to walk through. You see that it has become a portal, opening onto another realm of existence. At this point, pass through the portal into the elemental realm beyond.

The first time you do this, stop just inside the portal and simply look around. Let images rise in your mind the way they did when you imagined the standing stone. What does the realm of the element look like? What sounds, scents, and other perceptions come to you? Are there animals or other living things of any sort visible? If so, what do they look like, and what are they doing? Do they approach you or speak to you, and if the latter, what do they say?

When you have seen as much as you wish, or as much as the element appears to be willing to show you, go back through the portal into the Inner Grove. Face the symbol of the realm you just left, and imagine it shrinking back to its normal size. Return to the chair where your physical body is sitting, and sit down. Then allow the imagery of the Inner Grove to fade from your mind, stand up, and perform the closing half of the grove ceremony.

Afterward, make detailed notes on your scrying experiences in your Druid journal. Over the next few days, devote several sessions of meditation at least to the images, ideas, and events you experienced in your scrying. As imaginal experiences, these things will likely be packed with symbolic meanings that must be unpacked through meditation. Take your time, work through the experiences of the scrying one at a time, and finish the process before you do another scrying. You will find, as generations of mages have found before you, that one scrying opened up in meditation and thoroughly understood is worth twenty left unexplored.

The Uses of Scrying

It's best to scry each of the elements once to begin with, starting with air and going on in the same order you used to learn the invocations and banishings of the Gates. Each of these scryings is done the same way except for the last. When you scry Spirit Within, you don't need to get up out of your chair and face a portal; you yourself are the portal to Spirit Within. Instead, imagine yourself sitting in the same place as your material body. Let your imaginal self shrink and descend into your material body. Within your body, you find the inner landscape of your own microcosm. See what you find there, and when you are ready to return, imagine yourself expanding upward and outward until your imaginal body and your material body fill the same space, and then allow the imaginal body to fade from your mind's eye.

Once you've scried each of the seven elements once, you can scry them again in whatever order seems best to you. It's wise not to spend too much time on a single element, or neglect one of the elements completely, since scrying the elements will attune you to elemental forces and a scattershot approach risks imbalance. Still, this is one of the many dimensions of magical work where the personal equation is paramount. If you come to realize that you relate very poorly to one of the elements, doing a series of scryings of that element can be an effective way to bring yourself more into balance.

As you explore the elemental realms through scrying, you will find that the imaginal beings who inhabit them provide crucial dimensions of the experience. The modern world's materialist philosophy insists that such beings are "all in your imagination," but you'll find that the imaginal beings you encounter in scrying know things you don't, and behave in ways you can neither predict nor control. Treat them as real beings, with purposes and desires of their own, and you'll learn the most from them.

You can ask these beings, for example, to guide you in your journeys through the elemental realms. A good way to do this is to trace the elemental symbol clockwise, the invoking direction, and say words like this: "By the powers of [name of element] I ask for a faithful guide in this elemental realm." If a spirit approaches you, ask it to trace the same elemental symbol in the air. If it passes this test, you may safely accept its guidance. After it has shown you as much of the elemental realm as it chooses, ask it to take you back to your starting place, and when it does, trace the elemental symbol counterclockwise and say words like these: "By the powers of [element] I thank you. May the blessing of [element] always be with you." Then close the scrying as usual.

Magical lore gives many names to the beings of the elemental realms. One useful set comes from Welsh faery lore, which fuses Celtic and medieval magical traditions. The beings met beyond the Gate of the East are the *Tylwyth Teg* (pronounced "TUH-loo-uth TEG"), the light-elves; they wear red garments and teach magic to those who please them. The beings beyond the Gate of the West are the *Ellyllon* (pronounced "ELH-ulh-on"), the forest elves; they wear white garments, and will share wilderness lore and the secrets of herbs to those who earn their trust. The beings beyond the Gate of the South are the *Coblynau* (pronounced "KOB-luh-nye"), the dwarves, dwellers in mines and mountains who dress in drab colors. They have all the secrets of craftsmanship in their keeping, and will communicate these to apt pupils. The beings beyond the Gate of the North are the *Bwbachod* (pronounced "BOO-bakh-od"), the spirits of houses and fields; they wear brown garments, and teach the arts of farming and housekeeping to those who are diligent and patient.

The three realms of Spirit are inhabited by more powerful beings, the three great families of Welsh myth. The realm of Spirit Above is the home of the Plant Don (pronounced "plohnt DONN"), the children of the goddess Don. In the last age of the world they were ruled by Math son of Mathonwy; their rulers in this age of the world are Gwydion (pronounced "GWI-dee-on") son of Don—in Welsh, Gwydion ap Don—and his sister Arianrhod (pronounced "ah-ree-ANN-rhod") daughter of Don—in Welsh, Arianrhod ferch Ddon (pronounced "verkh THON"). The Plant Don are the regents of the Sun, the Star Logoi of Western occult tradition, and Welsh folklore assigns them homes among the stars. Even today, the Welsh call the Milky Way Caer Wydion, the Castle of Gwydion, or Caer Arianrhod, the Castle of Arianrhod. Some of the lore of the Plant Don may be found in the fourth branch of the *Mabinogion*.

The realm of Spirit Below is the home of the Plant Annwn (pronounced "plohnt ANN-oon"), the children of Annwn, the realm of the dead and also the source of all life. In the last age of the world they were ruled by Arawn; their rulers in this age of the world are Gwyn ap Nudd (pronounced "GWUN app NEETH") and his wife Creiddylad ferch Ludd (pronounced "CREY-thu-lad verkh LEETH"). In Welsh tradition, lakes are gateways to Annwn, and maidens called *Gwragedd Annwn* (pronounced goo-RAG-eth ANN-oon"), "women of Annwn," are said to come from beneath the waters of lakes bearing strange gifts. The Lady of the Lake in Arthurian legend, who gave Arthur the magical sword Excalibur, was one of these. Some of the lore of the Plant Annwn can be found in the first branch of the *Mabinogion*.

The realm of Spirit Within is the home of the Plant Llyr (pronounced "plohnt LHUR"), the children of the god Llyr. In the last age of the world they were ruled by Bran ap Llyr, called Bran the Blessed; their rulers in this age of the world are Manawyddan ap Llyr (pronounced "man-a-WUTH-ann app LHUR") and his wife Rhiannon ferch Hefeydd Hen (pronounced "rhee-ANN-on verkh HEV-eyth HEN"). The Plant Llyr are the archetypal forms of humanity, and their struggles, triumphs, and tragedies echo the fundamental patterns of human existence; they also represent particular energies within the human body that can be encountered and awakened by a variety of magical practices. Some of the lore of the Plant Llyr can be found in the second and third branches of the *Mabinogion*.

These beings should be approached carefully and with due respect. Strictly speaking, they are not elemental beings at all, but belong to the class of mighty spirits that different traditions call angels, intelligences, or devas. Very often they test newcomers to their realms before revealing any of their secrets, and the tests are not always obvious ones. Those who pass their tests and earn their regard, though, can receive magical teachings of great power. The Plant Don and Plant Annwn govern the two great currents of energy that shape the cosmos of Druid magic, and the Plant Llyr govern the energies of the human body—the alchemical vessel where these two currents fuse to create the lunar current, the creative power of Awen.

Awakening the Two Currents

A final dimension of work that can be done within the sacred space established by the grove ritual focuses on these currents. The solar, telluric, and lunar currents are much more than mere theoretical factors in Druid magic. Magical workings can summon the first two and create the third. Your body, the portal of Spirit Within, provides the context where this work takes place first; once you have accomplished it within your body, the same dance of nwyfre can then be set in motion in wider circles around you until it encompasses the whole world.

These workings—the active workings for Spirit Below, Above, and Within—are at least potentially much more intensive than any of the earlier rituals in this book, and so require more careful preparation. Before you start planning, cast an Ogham reading to make sure you are ready, just as you would if you were performing any other ritual working. If you get an unfavorable reading, keep working with the practices covered in earlier sections of this book for at least two weeks before you try again. This is a serious step, and it should not be rushed.

Once your Ogham sticks or cards tell you that you are ready to proceed, schedule your invocation of the telluric current at least a week in the future. It should be performed at the time of Dewaint, between midnight and 3:00 AM, when the telluric current is strongest. Choose a night when you can perform the ritual during this time without any risk of interruption. Schedule your invocation of the solar current at least a week later, during the time of Nawn, between noon and 3:00 PM—this is the time when the solar current is strongest.

Before you perform the ritual to invoke the telluric current, spend a week on meditations on Spirit Below. During these meditations, explore what myth and legend have to say about the underworld and the presence of spirits below us, and try to grasp what those mythic symbols are trying to communicate. Why are the spirits of the dead associated with *below,* and not some other direction? You don't have to come up with an answer. The important thing is that you grapple with the questions.

When the night of the working arrives, prepare the space for an ordinary grove ceremony. Before you begin, purify your body by washing in cold water. If you can bathe in a river or stream, this is best, but an ordinary tub will do, or even a sink and a washcloth. Once you have washed, put on your ritual garments, light the candle and incense, and begin the grove ceremony shortly after midnight. Perform the grove ceremony in the usual way. When you do the Sphere of Protection, ask each of the elements to help you make contact with the telluric current, and banish all obstacles to that contact from yourself and the grove. When you finish opening the grove, take your seat in the north, relax your body, and spend a few minutes doing color breathing with orange, the color of Spirit Below.

At this point turn your attention to the land beneath your feet. Imagine currents of energy flowing up from the center of the Earth, channeled through veins of metal in the rocks, surging up through the roots of trees, bringing vitality to all living things. Feel yourself as part of the biosphere, one small manifestation of the life force of the planet.

Rise to your feet and go to the north of the altar, facing south. Trace the heather pentagram over the altar, starting from the bottom point and going clockwise, as shown in Figure 5-3. As you do this, imagine the pentagram as though your fingers were drawing it in the air. There are at least three ways to handle this imagery. You can see the lines of the pentagram drawn in orange light, like the elemental emblems in the Sphere of Protection. You can also draw on Ogham symbolism and see them as five straight heather boughs interwoven in the form of a pentagram.

Finally, you can take the Ogham symbolism one step further and include the Ogham trees pointed out by the other four points of the pentagram. Look at the picture of the heather pentagram on the dolmen arch in Figure 2-5. The bottom point touches *U* for Ur, the heather, but the other points have trees of their own: Huath the hawthorn, Ngetal the reed, Luis the rowan, and Tinne the holly, in order

Figure 5-3   Tracing the Heather Pentagram

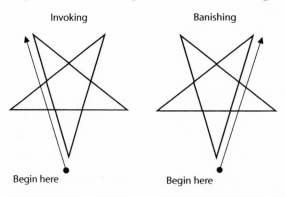

clockwise around the pentagram. To include all of these, imagine a straight heather bough extending from the bottom point to the upper left point, a hawthorn branch going from there to the right, a reed straight across from right to left, a rowan bough going from the left hand point to the upper right point, and a branch of holly slanting down from the upper right point to the bottom point. Of course, you need to know what all five of these look like! This is the strongest form of the heather pentagram, because each of the Ogham trees of this pentagram also belongs to the telluric current, and their symbolism helps bring it through in a more complete form.

Once you have traced the pentagram, imagine the current of life force from within the Earth surging up into the grove like cool water from a spring. Feel its invigorating and vitalizing power. Breathe it into yourself with each inbreath until every cell of your body is singing with the sheer joy of being alive. Concentrate on this as intently as possible for as long as you can.

When you are ready to close, trace the heather pentagram in reverse, starting from the bottom point and going counterclockwise. Imagine your fingers erasing the imagery you established when you drew the invoking form, whether that took the form of orange light, heather branches, or the five Ogham trees of the pentagram. Then sit down again in the north, relax your body, and pay attention to your breath for a few moments before closing.

After you have completed this ritual, prepare for the corresponding solar ritual. Devote the week before the solar current invocation to intensive daily meditations, taking the concept of Spirit descending from above as your theme. In these meditations, explore why it is that so many spiritual traditions think of the spiritual as above the material, why heaven is in the sky and mystics talk of the higher self and higher levels of being. Why *above,* and not below, ahead, beside, beyond, or in some other direction? You need not come up with an answer to these questions; what matters is that you wrestle with them, so that the symbolism of the ritual finds resonances in your own inner life.

Begin the ritual after purifying yourself with cold water and dressing in your ritual garments. Perform the grove ceremony in the ordinary way. In the Sphere of Protection, ask the elements to help you contact the solar current, and banish all obstacles to that contact from yourself and the grove. When you finish the opening, sit in the north, relax your body, and do purple color breathing to attune with Spirit Above.

At this point turn your attention to the Sun high above you, pouring down its rays on the Earth. Imagine light descending from the Sun through the vast reaches of outer space to your grove. Picture the planets in their orbits receiving the Sun's light and passing it on again. Sense all of space filled with the radiance and influence of the Sun.

Rise to your feet and go to the north of the altar, facing south. Trace the oak pentagram above the altar with the first two fingers of your right hand, starting with the top point and going clockwise, as shown in Figure 5-4. As with the heather pentagram, you can imagine the lines of the oak pentagram as pure purple light, as five branches of oak interwoven into a pentagram, or as branches of the five Ogham trees marked by the points of the pentagram. These are Duir the oak, Eadha the aspen, Nuin the ash, Gort the ivy, and Onn the gorse respectively, going clockwise around the pentagram from the top point. This last is the strongest form, but any of the three may be used with good effect.

Figure 5-4 Tracing the Oak Pentagram

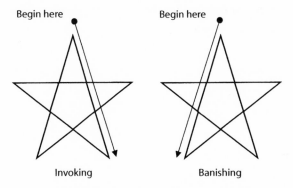

Begin here   Begin here

Invoking   Banishing

Once you trace and imagine the pentagram, picture in your mind's eye a beam of light descending from the Sun to your grove. Feel its warmth and the clarity it gives to your mind and imagination. As you breathe in each breath, imagine yourself drawing the light into your body until every cell is blazing with solar light. Concentrate on this as intently as possible.

When you are ready to close, trace the oak pentagram in reverse, starting from the top point and going counterclockwise. Imagine your fingers erasing the imagery you established when you drew the invoking form, whether that took the form of purple light, oak branches, or the five Ogham trees of the pentagram. Then sit down again in the north, relax your body, and pay attention to your breath for a few moments before you perform the closing.

Once you have done each of these ceremonies once, wait for at least a month before doing either one again. They can catalyze powerful changes in yourself and your life, and it's wise to let those changes run their course before bringing more of either current to bear on yourself. In the meantime, continue your basic practices and, if divination favors it, plan and perform a working or two for practical purposes, using the rituals given earlier in this chapter. Once you have established contact with the solar and telluric currents, the results of even simple magical workings may surprise you.

Part Two: The Practice of Druid Magic

CHAPTER 6
The Art of Enchantment

The magical workings presented so far in this book have used very little in the way of equipment. This follows a longstanding habit in the Druid Revival community. In the Ancient Order of Druids in America (AODA), for example, the only Druid gear any member needs to have, even at the highest degree of initiation, are a robe, a nemyss, a colored cord belt, a colored stone, a small cloth or leather bag, a knife, a cauldron, and a staff or wand. Other traditional Druid orders have similar ha-bits when it comes to magical hardware. Compared to many other magical traditions, this is a fairly sparse toolkit, and next to the splendid Victorian clutter of nineteenth-century magical orders such as the Hermetic Order of the Golden Dawn, it may seem quite ascetic.

Still, the art of enchanting tools and other material objects has an important place in Druid magic. The handful of working tools Druids use in their magical practices can be filled with nwyfre and linked to the great currents and cycles of the cosmos, so that magical work done with the tools echoes outward into a wider world. The same thing can be done to the Druid's own body, enaid, and mind for exactly the same reasons. Both these steps, in turn, lead to one of the core dimensions of Druid magic, the use of enchantment to bring spiritual powers into manifestation throughout the world of matter—literally, the reenchantment of the world.

A Circle of Stones

A basic technique you have already learned offers a good way to begin work on the art of enchantment. Back in chapter 4, you learned how to charge a stone with a magical intention. This simple method of enchantment has long been taught to novices in the AODA, but one of its applications links to a practice common in the Druid community since the late eighteenth century.

Iolo Morganwg, the innovative Welsh Druid responsible for most of the basic elements of classic Druid Revival ritual, established the custom of opening Druid groves inside a stone circle. When it wasn't possible to use one of the ancient circles such as Stonehenge or Avebury, or one of the newly built ones that his work inspired in Wales and elsewhere, Iolo simply brought a pocketful of small stones and marked out the ritual circle with those. The epochal ceremony on London's Primrose Hill in 1792 that launched Iolo's public Druid career took place within such a circle of stones.

Since then, Druids of many traditions have used this sort of portable stone circle in their rituals to define and anchor ritual space. Regular use in Druid ritual will enchant these stones, so that the simple act of setting them in a circle will begin the process of establishing the grove and awakening its energies. This process can be quickened, though, by deliberately enchanting the stones with this intention. The correspondences given in Table 6-1 provide the symbolic framework for this working.

Table 6-1 Correspondences for Stone Circle Rituals

Station	Color	Emblem	Welsh Deity	Irish Deity	Saint/Angel
Samhuinn	Violet	Cauldron	Ceridwen	Morrigan	Saint Peter Apostle
Alban Arthuan	White	Crown	Hu	Dagda	Archangel Uriel
Imbolc	Brown	Circle of candles	Ana	Brighid	Saint Brigid of Kildare
Alban Eiler	Red	Dragon	Coel	Aengus	Archangel Raphael
Belteinne	Sky blue	Hirlas (mead horn)	Elen	Eriu	Saint John Evangelist
Alban Heruin	Yellow	Three Rays	Beli	Lugh	Archangel Michael
Lughnasadh	Green	Fiery wheel	Sul	Tailtiu	Saint Mary Magdalene
Alban Elued	Royal blue	Silver branch	Esus	Mannanan	Archangel Gabriel

Start by choosing eight stones, one for each of the Stations of the Wheel of Life. Any stone that appeals to you, from plain pebbles to carefully chosen semiprecious stones, can be used. Wash them in fresh running water to cleanse them of unwanted nwyfre, and expose them to sunlight for at least an hour. Once you have done this, decide which of them corresponds to each Station of the Wheel, and mark them with the emblem of the Station, or in any other way you choose. You may also want to get a bag of cloth or leather to hold the eight stones. The only other preparations for the working are those you need to open a grove.

Open in the usual way, with the stone you've chosen for Samhuinn at the center of the altar; you won't need the others until later. In the Sphere of Protection, call upon the elements to bless and protect your grove and add their power to your working, and banish any influences that might hinder your work. Once you open the grove, take your seat in the north, and use violet color breathing to attune yourself to the energies of Samhuinn. Enter into meditation for a time, with Samhuinn as the theme. Contemplate the autumn sunlight, the lengthening nights, the fading leaves, and everything else nature does at that time of year in the region where you live. Imagine the grove filled with the nwyfre of Samhuinn.

When you are ready, breathe it all into yourself through your solar plexus in the form of violet light. Then rise and go to the altar. Pick up the stone with the index fingers and thumbs of both hands, and allow all the violet light and the presence of Samhuinn in you to flow into it. Say words such as these: "In the name of Ceridwen I enchant you, creature of stone, with the enchantment of Samhuinn. Embrace that enchantment, reflect it, and radiate it into the world. Yours is the Station of Samhuinn in the circle of my grove. Keep watch in the northwest." Pick up the stone again, carry it to the northwest edge of the grove, and set it on the ground there.

Return to the center and pause for a time, paying attention to the nwyfre of the ritual, then begin the grove closing ceremony. When you have finished the closing, pick up the stone and put it away—in your bag, if you have one, or in whatever other place you choose to keep your grove stones—before you clear away anything else from the grove. When you next perform a grove ceremony, place the Samhuinn stone in the northwest after you have set out everything else needed for the ceremony, but before you begin it.

You will need to perform seven more ceremonies of the same kind, changing the names and details as needed, and enchanting one stone in each ceremony. If you wish, you can do one ritual on each of the eight holy days, enchanting the stone for each Station of the Wheel of Life on its corresponding day; this produces a very powerful set of stones. It's best to proceed around the Wheel clockwise from Samhuinn, so that you enchant the stone for Alban Arthuan next and the one for Alban Elued last. Each time, when you enchant a

Figure 6-1   The Eight Stones and the Grove

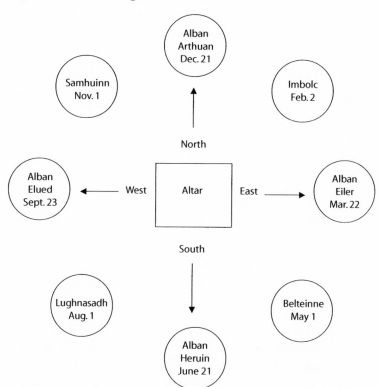

stone, put it in its position around the outside of the grove, as shown in Figure 6-1, and use it to mark out the grove in your workings thereafter. When you finish the process, you will have eight enchanted stones to define the circle of your grove in ritual, and the strength of your workings will increase accordingly.

If you want to use some other number of stones beside eight, you can certainly do so. Iolo Morganwg's stone circles had nineteen stones, modeled on the ancient stone circle at Boscawen-Un in Cornwall. Some modern Druid orders use stone circles with twelve stones, others use thirteen, and if you belong to one of these orders or simply want to experiment with a different number, choose an appropriate symbolism and go to work.

Making a permanent circle of standing stones is a more magically intensive process, because stones set up in the Earth attract the solar and telluric currents and, under the right circumstances, can give birth to the lunar current. A way of handling the magical dimensions of this very traditional Druid practice is covered in chapter 8 of this book.

The Druid Wand

The basic method of enchantment used to make your circle of stones has many other uses in practical magic, but you should also learn how to do more intensive forms of enchantment. One of these draws on the solar and telluric currents and can be used to enchant the first of the three principal working tools of the Druid mage, the wand.

Wands and staves of various kinds appear frequently in Druid hands in the old Irish legends, and of course mages around the world have used wands of various kinds for many thousands of years. In the system of magic taught in this book, the wand is an essential working tool, the instrument used to direct and channel nwyfre in ritual.

Your first task, of course, is finding, buying, or making a wand that suits your needs and tastes. It should certainly be made of wood, should fit comfortably in your hand, and should be short enough that you can make ritual gestures and trace figures in the air in your usual working space without hitting the furniture or the ceiling. Other than those simple rules, though, the details are up to you. The wand I use most often for Druid magic—I have more than a dozen wands in all—is around 14 inches long, was crafted from maple by a professional wandmaker, and has a quartz crystal point set into the business end, but I have used wands ranging in size from 6 inches to 8 feet, and in complexity from branches picked up in the forest to intricate pieces worked with seven metals and magically charged semiprecious stones. Each one has its own energy, and the complicated ones are not necessarily better.

Once you have your wand, wash it in cold running water, preferably in a stream or river, and leave it in direct sunlight for at least an hour to cleanse it of unwanted nwyfre. You will need to make preparations for an ordinary grove ceremony. If you want to do so, you can enchant your wand on one of the eight festivals of the Druid year, or on some other day that is special to you, but this is not required.

Place the wand on the center of the altar, and set your grove stones around the outside of your ritual space, before you begin the grove opening. Open in the usual way. In the Sphere of Protection, call on the elements to fill the wand with their power, and banish any hindrance to the enchantment from the wand, the working, and the grove. When you finish the opening and take your seat, use white color breathing—the symbolic color of nwyfre—to prepare for the meditation, and then meditate on the wand as a symbol and a magical working tool.

When you are ready, rise and approach the altar. Say words like these: "O my wand, you have been crafted from the body of a tree that you may share in the work of Druid magic. Before you may take up that work, you must make a journey through the four elements."

Circle around to the east side of the altar, facing the center, and say, "Arise, and enter the realm of air." Pick up the wand and move it back and forth through the incense smoke from the air cauldron, so that every part receives some of the smoke. Say words like these: "In the name of Hu and by the powers of the realm of air I purify you and strengthen you for your work." Concentrate on the idea that the incense smoke is cleansing the wand and filling it with the powers of the element of air. When it feels right, return the wand to the center of the altar.

Circle around to the south side of the altar, facing the center, and say, "Arise, and enter the realm of fire." Pick up the wand and move it just above the flame in the fire cauldron, so that every part receives heat and light from the flame. Say words like these: "In the name of Sul and by the powers of the realm of fire I purify you and strengthen you for your work." Concentrate on the idea that the heat of the flame is cleansing the wand and filling it with the powers of the element of fire. When it feels right, return the wand to the center of the altar.

Circle around to the west side of the altar, facing the center, and say, "Arise, and enter the realm of water." Pick up the wand and hold it above the water cauldron, then dip the fingers of one hand into the water and sprinkle the wand with it, so that every part receives some of the water. Say words like these: "In the name of Esus and by the powers of the realm of water I purify you and strengthen you for your work." Concentrate on the idea that the water is cleansing the wand and filling it with the powers of the element of water. When it feels right, return the wand to the center of the altar.

Circle around to the north side of the altar, facing the center, and say, "Arise, and enter the realm of earth." Pick up the wand and hold it above the earth cauldron, and sprinkle some of the salt or earth from the cauldron onto it, so that every part of it receives some. Say words like these: "In the name of Elen and by the powers of the realm of earth I purify you and strengthen you for your work." Concentrate on the idea that the salt or earth is cleansing the wand and filling it with the powers of the element of earth. When it feels right, return the wand to the center of the altar.

Turn your attention to the land beneath you, and imagine the telluric current rising up from the heart of the Earth. Say words like these: "When the four material elements are in balance, the element of spirit appears in their midst." Pick up the wand, and use it to trace an invoking heather pentagram over the altar, saying, "I invoke Spirit Below. Let the telluric current arise and bless this wand." Place the wand on the altar, and imagine a shaft of silver light rising from far beneath you to shine on the wand. Make this image as vivid as possible, and maintain it for several minutes at least.

Release the image, then, and turn your attention to the sky above you. Imagine the solar current cascading down through space from the Sun. Pick up the wand, feeling the presence of the telluric current within it, and use it to trace an invoking oak pentagram over the altar, saying words like these: "I invoke Spirit Above. Let the solar current descent and bless this wand." Place the wand on the altar, and imagine a shaft of golden light shining down from infinite space above you to illumine the wand. Make this image as vivid as possible, and maintain it for several minutes at least.

Pick up the wand again and hold it vertically with both hands above the altar, in the middle of the space where you traced the two pentagrams. Say words like these: "From above to below, from below to above, the two currents are awakened. I invoke Spirit Within. Let the lunar current be born within this wand and fill it with the power of Awen."

Imagine the golden solar current and the silver telluric current both shining into the wand at once, and then see them fuse into pure white light, the color of lightning, in and around the wand. Imagine the disk of the Moon surrounding your hands and the shining wand. Once again, make this image as vivid as possible, and hold it for several minutes at least.

Then hold the wand in your right hand, and say, "I take upon myself the power, the responsibility, and the burden of this wand. The power to awaken and direct nwyfre in accord with my intention; the responsibility to use that power well and wisely, in harmony with the great pattern of all things; and the burden of bearing the consequences if I fail to do so."

At this point the wand is enchanted, and the best way to make the enchantment lasting is to use the wand in its new role as soon as possible. For this reason, holding the wand in one hand, perform the Sphere of Protection ritual a second time. Trace the symbols with the wand, but only in the invoking form, and ask the elements to confirm and strengthen the powers of the wand. When you have finished, proceed to the grove closing ceremony.

Once you enchant it, your wand can be used any time you perform the Sphere of Protection or the full Grove Ceremony. Use it to trace elemental symbols and pentagrams in the air, and to direct and channel nwyfre for any purpose— for example, when charging water or anything else in a magical working, you can direct the nwyfre through the wand rather than through your hands. With practice, you will find that using your wand in this way improves the intensity and focus of the nwyfre you can place in a material substance. Expect to learn other uses for your wand as you continue to learn and practice magic.

The Cauldron

The ritual for consecrating the wand shows how the elements and the solar and telluric currents can be brought into the work of enchantment. The eight Stations of the Wheel of Life can also be used in much the same way. The second of the three primary working tools of the Druid mage, the cauldron, can be enchanted in this way, using the oak and heather pentagrams.

In the Welsh traditions from which the Druid Revival draws so much of its symbolism, magical cauldrons play an important role. At the center of the Druid teaching of the three circles of manifestation—Abred, the realm of plant, animal, and human existence in the world of nature; Gwynfydd, the realm of illumined existence beyond the human level; and Ceugant, the realm of absolute unity that no created being can traverse—stands the Cauldron of Annwn. This cauldron is the reservoir of raw nwyfre at the heart of existence, the place where souls are born, and where souls who utterly fail to grasp the lessons of Abred return and dissolve back into raw nwyfre.

Scarcely less important in Druid symbolism is the cauldron of Ceridwen, the wise old alchemist goddess in the legend of Taliesin. Ceridwen's cauldron held a brew containing all the wisdom in the world, and had to be kept bubbling for a year and a day. Among other things, this cauldron represents the Druid tradition itself, since this latter is brimful of wisdom and embraces the whole circle of the seasons.

The cauldron of the Druid mage reflects both these mythic cauldrons, but it also has a practical role in Druid magic. It serves as a reservoir of all the different forms and patterns of nwyfre needed in magical work. The Druid mage can draw any kind of nwyfre he or she wishes from the cauldron—

the forces of the elements, the Stations of the Wheel, the Ogham fews, and every other power used in Druid magic are all there. To put them there requires enchantment, and the invocations of the eight Stations of the Wheel are a suitable method for this work.

The first step in providing yourself with such a magical cauldron, of course, is getting the physical cauldron itself. Any cauldron-shaped vessel small enough to fit on top of your altar will serve. The cauldron I use for Druid magic is made of cast iron, about 5 inches across, with three stubby legs underneath; I found it in a cookware store in a display of cast-iron pots and pans. Other Druids I know use cauldrons of brass, pottery, and glass, and all of these work well.

Once you have your cauldron, wash it thoroughly in cold running water, preferably in a stream or river, and leave it in direct sunlight for at least an hour to cleanse it of unwanted nwyfre. You will also need to make preparations for an ordinary grove ceremony. If you want to do so, you can enchant your cauldron on one of the eight festivals of the Druid year, or on some other day that is special to you, but this is not required.

Set your grove stones around the edge of your ritual space, place the cauldron on the center of the altar, and have your wand on the altar as well, before you begin the grove opening. Open in the usual way. In the Sphere of Protection, trace the elemental symbols with your wand; call on the elements to fill the cauldron with their power, and banish any hindrance to the enchantment from the cauldron, the working, and the grove. When you finish the opening and take your seat, use blue color breathing—the color of gwyar—to prepare for the meditation, and then meditate on the cauldron as a symbol and a magical working tool.

When you are ready, rise and approach the altar. Say words like these: "O my cauldron, you have been made from the substance of the Earth that you may share in the work of Druid magic. Before you may take up that work, you must make a journey through the four elements."

Circle around to the east side of the altar, facing the center, and say, "Arise, and enter the realm of air." Pick up the cauldron and move it back and forth through the incense smoke, so that every part receives some of the smoke. Say words like these: "In the name of Hu and by the powers of the realm of air I purify you and strengthen you for your work." Concentrate on the idea that the incense smoke is cleansing the cauldron and filling it with the powers of the element of air. When it feels right, return the cauldron to the center of the altar.

Circle around to the south side of the altar, facing the center, and say, "Arise, and enter the realm of fire." Pick up the cauldron and move it just above the flame, so that every part receives heat and light from the fire. Say words like these: "In the name of Sul and by the powers of the realm of fire I purify you and strengthen you for your work." Concentrate on the idea that the heat of the flame is cleansing the cauldron and filling it with the powers of the element of fire. When it feels right, return the cauldron to the center of the altar.

Circle around to the west side of the altar, facing the center, and say, "Arise, and enter the realm of water." Pick up the cauldron and hold it above the water, then dip the fingers of one hand into the water and sprinkle the cauldron with it, so that every part receives some of the water. Say words like these: "In the name of Esus and by the powers of the realm of water I purify you and strengthen you for your work." Concentrate on the idea that the water is cleansing the cauldron and filling it with the powers of the element of water. When it feels right, return the cauldron to the center of the altar.

Circle around to the north side of the altar, facing the center, and say, "Arise, and enter the realm of earth." Pick up the cauldron and hold it above the earth cauldron, and sprinkle some of the salt or earth onto it, so that every part of it receives some. Say words like these: "In the name of Elen and by the powers of the realm of earth I purify you and strengthen you for your work." Concentrate on the idea that the salt or earth is cleansing the cauldron and filling it with the powers of the element of earth. When it feels right, return the cauldron to the center of the altar, where it will remain for the rest of the working.

Much of the rest of the ritual depends on the time of year when you perform this rite, because you need to start by invoking the current Station of the telluric current, and then proceed around the Wheel from there. You will be drawing a total of eight pentagrams, and facing in eight directions. The pentagrams are always drawn in the same way and the same order: the heather pentagram from the bottom point first, then the two heather pentagrams starting with the left-hand points, then the oak pentagram starting on the upper left point, then the oak pentagram starting on the top point, then the oak pentagrams starting on the two right-hand points, then the heather pentagram starting on the lower right point. On the other hand, the Stations you invoke, the words you say, and the directions you face, all change depending on the season.

For example, if you are enchanting your cauldron between November 1 and December 20, the solar current at that time is flowing through the Station of Samhuinn and the telluric current through Belteinne. You would begin this phase of the working by moving clockwise around the altar until you stand in the northwest, facing the cauldron on the altar and, beyond it, the stone representing Belteinne. If you are doing the working at a different time of the year, start with whatever Station holds the telluric current, facing across the altar toward the stone that corresponds to that Station. A glance at Figure 6-1 will make this easier to follow.

Next, using your wand, trace an invoking heather pentagram, starting with the lowermost point, in the air above the cauldron. Hold the tip of your wand at the lower point of the pentagram, and invoke the Station corresponding to the festival opposite the one you celebrated most recently. In the example of a ritual done just after Samhuinn, you might use words such as these: "I invoke the power of Belteinne, the festival of life and love. Let the power of Belteinne enter into this cauldron and bless it for its work." Move the tip of the wand down into the mouth of the cauldron. As you do so, imagine the energies of Belteinne (or whatever Station is aligned with the telluric current at the time you do the ritual) flowing into the tip of the wand and then down into the cauldron. Hold this for several minutes.

Now trace another invoking heather pentagram in the air above the altar, this time starting with the lower left point. Hold the tip of your wand at that point, and invoke the Station that will come next in the yearly cycle. In the example, this would be Alban Heruin, and you might use words such as these: "I invoke the power of Alban Heruin, the Station of the Sun in his summer glory. Let the power of Alban Heruin enter into this cauldron and bless it for its work." Then move the tip of the wand down into the mouth of the cauldron. As you do so, imagine the energies of Alban Heruin (or whatever Station is next at the time you do the ritual) flowing into the tip of the wand and then down into the cauldron. Hold this for several minutes.

Go on to the next Station—in the example, this would be Lughnasadh—and trace a heather pentagram beginning with the upper left point. Invoke the Station in your own words, move the wand from the point of the pentagram to the mouth of the cauldron, and transfer the power of the Station to the cauldron.

Go to the next Station—in the example, this would be Alban Elued. The fourth Station you invoke, whatever it may be, is the first Station in the realm of the solar current at the time you perform your ritual, and so you need trace an invoking oak pentagram instead of a heather pentagram, starting from the upper left point. Do the same things you did with the first three Stations you invoked. In the same way, invoke the next three Stations: face the appropriate direction, trace an oak pentagram for each one, and invoke the three other Stations of the Wheel that are in the solar realm at the time of your ritual. Finally, move around the altar to face the one remaining direction, and invoke the one remaining Station—in the example, this is Alban Eiler— with a heather pentagram traced clockwise from the lower right point.

Then touch the rim of the cauldron with your right hand. Say, "I take upon myself the power, the responsibility, and the burden of this cauldron. The power to draw forth from it nwyfre of every kind; the responsibility to use that power wisely and well, in harmony with the great pattern of all things; and the burden of bearing the consequences if I fail to do so."

Now, just as you did when you enchanted the wand, you need to use the powers you have called into the cauldron, in order to make the enchantment stable. This is best done by performing the Sphere of Protection ritual a second time, before you go on to the closing ceremony. Since the cauldron is a receptive tool rather than an active one, this is done in a different way.

Perform the Elemental Cross first in the usual way. Next, pick up the wand, and use the tip to draw the invoking symbol of air ϕ above the mouth of the cauldron. Imagine that the cauldron fills at once with yellow light that swirls and dances with all the energies of air. Dip the tip of the wand into the mouth of the cauldron, as though you were dipping a brush into a pot of paint. As you take the wand's tip out of the cauldron, imagine that all the yellow light comes with it, forming a sphere around the end of the wand. Go to the eastern edge of the grove and use that yellow light like paint, to draw the invoking symbol of air in the usual way. Call upon the powers of air to confirm and strengthen the powers of the cauldron. Don't trace the banishing symbol at all.

Return to the altar and, using the tip of the wand, draw the invoking symbol of fire $\triangle$ over the mouth of the cauldron. See the cauldron fill with red light full of the nwyfre of fire. Dip the end of the wand in the light, and use it to draw the invoking fire symbol in the south, then invoke the powers of fire. Do the same thing with the energies and invoking symbols of water ∇ and earth $\female$.

Next, use the circle of spirit $\bigcirc$ to invoke Spirit Below and Above, and the symbol of the three rays of light /|\, the traditional Druid emblem of Awen, to awaken Spirit Within in the cauldron. In each case, call on the elements to confirm and strengthen the powers of the cauldron. Proceed as usual to the Circulation of Light. When you have finished the second

Sphere of Protection, go on to the closing ceremony and perform this in the usual way.

Once you have enchanted your cauldron, it can be used as a reservoir of nwyfre to be shaped and directed by the wand. If you wish, you no longer need to use the four bowls or cauldrons of air, fire, water, and earth used in the grove opening ritual. You can simply draw each of these elements from the cauldron, dipping your wand into them and using each of them in turn to trace a circle around the grove, where you would otherwise pick up one of the elements and carry it around the grove. Your cauldron will always be full of the seven elements and the nwyfre of the eight Stations. It can also be filled with other forms of nwyfre in magical ritual. Working with the Ogham fews makes an excellent introduction to this side of Druid magic.

Preparation for Ogham Magic

Each of the twenty-five Ogham fews, as mentioned back in chapter 2, makes a connection between two of the Stations of the Wheel of Life. Each of these connections has its own special quality of nwyfre, with a more precise focus than the broad energies of the elements or the Stations of the Wheel. These form an essential part of the Druid mage's toolkit.

If you want to work magic for protection, for example, you can use the broad brush of the element of earth or the Station of Alban Heruin if you wish, since both of these have general protective powers. On the other hand, you can call on any one of five fews with more exact powers: Luis dispels delusion, Fearn invokes the protection of the gods and goddesses, Duir brings great strength, Straif imposes barriers that cannot be crossed, and Eadha shields you against hostility and misfortune. One or another of these may do much more for your specific needs than a more general protective working.

If you want to make use of the fews and their nwyfre, though, you need to understand them thoroughly and make contact with them on inner levels. As bare physical signs, scratches on a piece of wood or stone, they have no power. They function magically only when awakened as symbols of imaginal and formal realities, and this takes work.

The process began when you started doing Ogham divinations as a daily practice in chapter 3. By keeping up this practice, you already know quite a bit about the fews from seeing them reflected in the events of your daily life. Building on that foundation starts with meditation. Take each of the Ogham fews as a theme for meditation for at least three sessions, and as many more as you find useful.

If you wish to go beyond this, meditate on the correspondences of the fews listed in *The Druidry Handbook* or any other book of Ogham lore, taking each correspondence as a theme and exploring how it relates to the meaning of the few. This will give you a good grasp of the nature of each few. This will take around two years even if you meditate on one correspondence every day. It's a project worth pursuing when you decide you want to get into the deeper dimensions of the fews—I have done it, and the results were well worth the time it took—but this level of intensity is not needed to start using the fews in magic.

Scrying forms the next stage in your work with the Ogham fews. Each of the five *aicme,* or groups, of fews is assigned to one of the elements. The first aicme, from Beith to Saille, belongs to air; the second, from Huath to Quert, belongs to fire; the third, from Muin to Ruis, belongs to water;

the fourth, from Ailm to Ioho, belongs to earth, and the forfedha belong to spirit. You enter the realm of each few through the quarter of its element, imagining a portal there in place of the elemental sign you used in your first scryings.

The portal of Beith, in other words, is in the east, that of Duir in the south, that of Gort in the west, and that of Ioho in the north; the forfedha can be reached either above or below, as your intuition guides you. Place your chair so that it faces across the altar toward the direction of the portal. If you plan on scrying Beith, for example, your chair will be in the west, facing east across the altar. After you open the grove, sit in the west and practice color breathing, using the traditional colors of the fews from Table 6-2. Then meditate on Beith for a time, before imagining the Inner Grove and beginning your scrying, using the same approach you used in scrying the elements in the work of chapter 5.

Table 6-2   Colors of the Ogham Fews

First Aicme
Beith: White
Luis: Light gray
Nuin: Clear
Fearn: Red
Saille: Primrose yellow

Second Aicme
Huath: Deep violet
Duir: Black
Tinne: Dark gray
Coll: Brown
Quert: Mouse-brown

Third Aicme
Muin: Variegated
Gort: Sky blue
Ngetal: Grass green
Straif: Silver
Ruis: Dark red

Fourth Aicme
Ailm: Piebald
Onn: Dun
Ur: Red amber
Eadha: Rust red
Ioho: Very white

Forfedha
Koad: Many shades of green
Oir: Brilliant white
Uilleand: Yellow white
Phagos: Orange brown
Mór: Blue green

You can scry each few as soon as you finish meditating on it, or wait until you have meditated on all of them before you begin scrying them, as you wish. The scrying process will give you plenty of new themes for meditation since, just as you did when scrying the elements, you should plan on meditating on any symbols or ideas that surface during a scrying. A bit of traditional lore suggests that you should plan on spending three sessions in meditation for every one you devote to scrying. In my experience, this can be considered a bare minimum.

Ogham Pathworking

A final stage of preparation for Ogham magic, and one of the most powerful forms of imaginal work in its own right, is the art of Pathworking. This goes one step beyond scrying by putting the Ogham few in relationship to the two Stations of the Wheel it connects. When you do a Pathworking, you travel from one Station to another on an imaginal journey through an inner landscape established by the Ogham few.

This is not quite what many people in the occult community mean when they talk about Pathworking, and the difference needs to be understood clearly. To many occultists these days, a Pathworking is a guided visualization meant to be read aloud from a prepared script. The events of the experience are planned out ahead of time, and the people doing this sort of Pathworking imagine themselves going through the events and encountering the beings described to them. Work of this kind can be useful, especially for beginners, but it has serious limits and does little to develop your own ability to experience the imaginal world directly.

The approach to Pathworking used in Druid magic builds on the art of scrying instead. Start by preparing for scrying in the usual way, with the grove opening, Sphere of Protection, color breathing, and a brief meditation. Instead of imagining yourself in the Inner Grove, however, imagine yourself in one of the eight places listed in Table 6-3, corresponding to the eight Stations of the Wheel of Life. Imagine the place in the colors of the Station, and picture the emblem of the Station near the altar. Make all this imagery as clear and vivid as possible.

When you are ready, rise from the chair in your imagination, and go to the altar. Imagine yourself picking up the wand and tracing a pentagram to invoke the Station where you wish to start your Pathworking. As always, the pentagram you use and the point you start from will change depending on the season of the year. In your own words, invoke the powers of the Station, and ask that they watch over you as you travel the inner path to the Station you intend to reach at the end of your Pathworking.

For example, your first Pathworking would traditionally be from Alban Arthuan to Imbolc along the path of Beith, few of the birch tree. After the usual preparations, you would start this by imagining yourself high in the northern sky, surrounded on all sides by stars. The stars blaze white and gold, and a crown floats in the air above the altar. You imagine yourself rising and walking across a floor paved with stars toward the altar. If you were doing this Pathworking between Alban Elued and Samhuinn, let's say, you would invoke Alban Arthuan with an invoking heather pentagram, starting from the upper right corner and tracing the pentagram in a clockwise direction. You might then say words such as these: "In the name of Hu the Mighty, the great Druid god, I invoke the powers of Alban Arthuan to watch over me as I travel the path of Beith to the Station of Imbolc."

At this point, you would begin a scrying of Beith in the usual way. Unless you have been this way before, ask for a guide on the path, and ask your guide to lead you to the portal of the Station you intend to reach—in the example, Imbolc. Proceed as in any other scrying. When you get to the portal of the Station on the other end, thank your guide and imagine yourself entering into that Station. See it in the form given in Table 6-3, with the colors and emblem listed there. Imagine yourself walking up to the altar and tracing a pentagram to invoke the Station you have just reached. Once you have done this, thank the powers of the Station in your own words for welcoming you, take your seat in the grove, and begin the closing as usual.

In the example, for instance, you would imagine yourself entering into a cavern deep within the Earth, all in earth colors and black, with a circle of eight candles around the

Table 6-3 Inner Places of the Stations

Station	Colors	Emblem	Inner Place
Samhuinn	Violet and silver	Cauldron	A high mountain peak
Alban Arthuan	White and gold	Crown	A space in the northern stars
Imbolc	Brown and black	Circle of candles	A cavern within the earth
Alban Eiler	Indigo and red	Dragon	A stone chamber in a barrow
Belteinne	Sky blue and orange	Hirlas (mead horn)	A spring beside a tree
Alban Heruin	Red and yellow	Three rays	A stone circle on a plain
Lughnasadh	Gold and green	Fiery wheel	A circle of trees amid fields
Alban Elued	Leaf green and blue	Silver branch	A standing stone on a mound
Central Grove	All shades of green	Standing stone	A crossroads amid the forest

altar. You would approach the altar and invoke Imbolc with a heather pentagram, traced clockwise from the lower left point. You might then say, "In the name of Ana, the goddess of the Earth's deep places, I invoke the powers of the Station of Imbolc. Thank you for receiving me and giving me your hospitality." You would then take your seat in the grove, and close in the usual way.

Pathworking in this way is a potent magical technique. Few things will teach you as much about the Ogham fews, their relationship to the Stations, and the Wheel of Life as a whole. As you work your way through the whole set of fews, you will find that your ability to use them in magic and divination increases dramatically, and the guides who appear on the paths can teach you much about Druid magic.

It works best to start Pathworking with the Ogham fews by doing each few once in order, from Beith all the way to Mór. Koad alone of the fews does not stand for a path; it represents the Central Grove, and Pathworkings of Koad involve sitting in the Central Grove itself and seeing what entities come to meet you. This can be at least as complex as any inner journey! All the others give you a framework for a journey. Once you have traveled each few once, you can repeat the process, or focus on those fews you feel you need to understand better. You can also use a Pathworking of a particular few as part of a ritual working to invoke the few for magical purposes, as explained next.

Ogham in Practical Magic

Once you have meditated on a few and explored it in scrying, you have the connection with that few you need to use it in magic. A simple way to do this is to add a single Ogham few to the Sphere of Protection ritual. Start by choosing a few that corresponds to your intention—for example, Tinne to focus your energies on a goal, or Ailm to give you a clearer awareness of a situation. Begin the Sphere of Protection ritual in the usual way, and proceed all the way to the Gate of Spirit Above, asking the elements to further your intention as you invoke them, and banishing all obstacles to its fulfillment.

At the Gate of Spirit Within, though, the ritual changes. Be aware of the six elements around you in the usual way, and then draw the Ogham few in the air in front of you with the first two fingers of your right hand. Draw the vertical stem line of the few from bottom to top, and then draw the other lines on it. Imagine the lines drawn in colored light, using the traditional color of the few itself.

Imagine the few glowing in the air before you, and say words like the following: "By the light that was before the worlds, by the creative power of Awen, I trace the few [name of few]. By its power, [here state your intention aloud]." Hold the few clearly in your imagination for a time, then

Figure 6-2   Tracing an Ogham Few

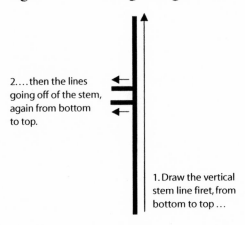

2....then the lines going off of the stem, again from bottom to top.

1. Draw the vertical stem line firet, from bottom to top ...

release the image and allow it to dissolve completely. Proceed to the Circulation of Light as usual.

Ogham magic can also be worked on a more intensive level, in a grove ritual. Prepare for the ritual by placing your chair so that you face the direction of the few across the altar, just as though you meant to scry the few. Your wand and cauldron should be on the altar. Open the grove in the usual way, take your seat in the grove, and spend several minutes doing color breathing using the traditional color of the few. Meditate on your intention and on how it relates to the few you have chosen. If you have explored the few in Pathworking, you can do another Pathworking along the same path at this point, to help yourself focus the energies of the few.

When you are ready, rise and go to the altar. Take your wand and dip its tip in the cauldron, and imagine the cauldron filling with light of the traditional color of the few. Then, as though your wand was a brush and the light was paint, draw the few in the air above the cauldron and see it shining there. Say words such as the following: "By the light that was before the worlds, by the creative power of Awen, I trace the few [name of few]. By its power, [state your intention here]." Pause for a time, concentrating on the image of the few.

Next, use the wand to trace an invoking heather pentagram over the altar, with the lowermost point just below the lower end of the stem. See the lines of the pentagram drawn in silver light. Say, "I invoke Spirit Below. Let the telluric current ascend and fill this few with its might." Imagine a shaft of silver light rising up from the heart of the Earth to shine into the few. Make this image as vivid as possible, and maintain it for several minutes at least.

Now use the wand to trace an invoking oak pentagram with its uppermost point just above the upper end of the few's vertical line. See the lines of the pentagram drawn in golden light. Say, "I invoke Spirit Above. Let the solar current descend and fill this few with its might." Imagine a shaft of golden light descending from far above you to shine into the few. Make this image as vivid as possible, and maintain it for several minutes at least.

Point the wand at the center of the few, and say, "From above to below, from below to above, the two currents are awakened. I invoke Spirit Within. Let the lunar current be born within this few and fill it with the power of Awen." Imagine the golden solar current and the silver telluric current both shining into the few at once, and then see them fuse into pure white light, the color of lightning, in and around the few. Imagine the disk of the Moon surrounding the few. Make this image as vivid as possible, hold it for several minutes at least, and then release it. When you are ready, close the ritual in the usual way.

The Crane Bag

According to Irish legend, one of the great treasures of the sea god Manannan mac Lir was a bag made of the skin of a magical crane. In his crane bag, the god stored the shears of the king of Alba (Scotland), the helmet of the king of Lochlann (Norway), the bones of Asail's pig, the belt and fish hook of Goibniu the smith god, and Manannan's own house. These may seem unlikely contents for a craneskin bag, but any Irish bard would have realized at once that the legend referred to the five forfedha of the Ogham alphabet. The "shears" are Koad, which looks like an open pair of scissors;

the "helmet" is Oir, which looks like an old Irish helmet seen from above; the "bones" are Uilleand, which looks like crossed bones; the "belt and fish hook" are Phagos, which looks like a hook hanging from a belt; and the "house" is Mór the sea, the proper house of a sea god.

Cranes have traditional links with writing, because migrating cranes look like letters drawn against the sky. The crane bag of Irish legend, then, is the Ogham alphabet itself. In modern Druid practice, by contrast, it is a small bag used to hold sacred objects, not unlike a Native American medicine pouch, and many Druids use one to hold their Ogham sticks. Worn on a strap or cord around the neck, so that the bag rests at the level of your heart or solar plexus, the crane bag also functions as what modern mages call a *lamen*—a symbolic object worn on the chest that represents your essential spiritual aspirations.

The first step in equipping yourself with a crane bag is to get a bag of cloth or leather just large enough to hold your set of Ogham sticks, or any other objects you intend to put in it. The color, shape, and design of the bag are up to you, but it should have a strap or cord that allows you to hang it around your neck. If you wish, it may have a Druid symbol on the front.

Once you have your crane bag, leave it in direct sunlight for at least an hour to cleanse it of unwanted nwyfre. If it can be washed in cold running water without damage—most leather and many cloth bags can't be—by all means do so. You will also need to make preparations for an ordinary grove ceremony. If you want to do so, you can enchant your crane bag on one of the festivals of the Druid year, or on some other day that is special to you, but this is not required.

Set your grove stones around the edge of your ritual space, and have your cauldron and wand on the altar. Your crane bag goes at the center of the altar. Open the grove in the usual way. In the Sphere of Protection, trace the elemental symbols with your wand; call on the elements to fill the crane bag with their power, and banish any hindrance to the enchantment from the crane bag, the working, and the grove. When you finish the opening and take your seat, use green color breathing—the color of the Druid element calas—to prepare for the meditation, and then meditate on the crane bag as a symbol and a magical working tool.

When you are ready, rise and approach the altar. Say words like these: "O my crane bag, you have been made from (here say something about the substance from which it is made) that you may share in the work of Druid magic. Before you may take up that work, you must make a journey through the four elements."

Circle around to the east side of the altar, facing the center, and say, "Arise, and enter the realm of air." Pick up the crane bag and move it back and forth through the incense smoke, so that every part receives some of the smoke. Say words like these: "In the name of Hu and by the powers of the realm of air I purify you and strengthen you for your work." Concentrate on the idea that the incense smoke is cleansing the crane bag and filling it with the powers of the element of air. When it feels right, return the bag to the center of the altar.

Circle around to the south side of the altar, facing the center, and say, "Arise, and enter the realm of fire." Pick up the crane bag and move it above the flame, so that every part receives heat and light from the fire; be careful not to let it actually contact the flame, however! Say words like these: "In the name of Sul and by the powers of the realm of fire I purify you and strengthen you for your work." Concentrate on the idea that the heat of the flame is cleansing the crane bag and filling it with the powers of the element of fire. When it feels right, return the bag to the center of the altar.

Circle around to the west side of the altar, facing the center, and say, "Arise, and enter the realm of water." Pick up the crane bag and hold it above the water, then dip the fingers of one hand into the water and sprinkle the crane bag with it, so that every part receives some of the water. Say words like these: "In the name of Esus and by the powers of the realm of water I purify you and strengthen you for your work." Concentrate on the idea that the water is cleansing the crane bag and filling it with the powers of the element of water. When it feels right, return the bag to the center of the altar.

Circle around to the north side of the altar, facing the center, and say, "Arise, and enter the realm of earth." Pick up the crane bag and hold it above the earth cauldron, and sprinkle some of the salt or earth onto it, so that every part of it receives some. Say words like these: "In the name of Elen and by the powers of the realm of earth I purify you and strengthen you for your work." Concentrate on the idea that the salt or earth is cleansing the crane bag and filling it with the powers of the element of earth. When it feels right, return the crane bag to the center of the altar.

Pause, and then pick up your wand. Touch the crane bag with the tip of the wand, and say, "Receive the blessing of the receptive powers of the cosmos, that you may manifest all the powers of the telluric current." Imagine nwyfre flowing from the wand into the crane bag, filling it with power. When it feels right, put the wand down, and pick up the crane bag. Touch it to the rim of the cauldron, and say, "Receive the blessing of the active powers of the cosmos, that you may contain all the powers of the solar current." Imagine nwyfre flowing from the cauldron into the crane bag, filling it with power. When it feels right, put the crane bag down.

Then take the crane bag and put it around your neck so that it hangs at the level of your heart. Say, "I take upon myself the power, the responsibility, and the burden of this crane bag. The power to wield nwyfre; the responsibility to use that power wisely and well, in harmony with the great pattern of all things; and the burden of bearing the consequences if I fail to do so."

At this point your crane bag is fully enchanted. As you did with your other working tools, your next step is to perform a Sphere of Protection ritual using only the invoking forms of the elemental symbols. Use your cauldron as the source of elemental energies, as you did after enchanting it, and use your wand to trace the circles and the elemental symbols. Your crane bag remains in its place on your chest. As you invoke each of the seven elements, ask the elemental powers in your own words to confirm and strengthen the power of the crane bag. Once you have finished, close in the usual way.

Weaving Your Own Enchantments

As you finish the work outlined in this chapter, you will wield the three working tools of the Druid mage together for the first time. At this point the possibilities open before you come close to infinity, and one of the major challenges you face is that of deciding what to do with your skills at the art of enchantment.

Other Working Tools

One practical and traditional use for enchantment is the creation of other working tools to fit the particular needs of your own magical path. Anything you use in a magical setting can be enchanted to make it a better channel for your intentions. Druids who practice herbal magic, for example, commonly enchant the knife they use to cut herbs, the mortar and pestle they use to powder them, and other pieces of equipment, while those who practice different kinds of divination often enchant their divining tools. If you travel in the wilderness, a magical staff is an obvious and useful accessory. Here as so often in magic, the possibilities are limited only by your imagination and your willingness to do the work.

Talismans

Another valuable use of enchantment is the art of making and using talismans. A talisman is a physical object filled with nwyfre and charged with a specific intention. Once charged, it sends the pattern of its intentionality out through the nwyfre night and day until and unless you disenchant it. This persistent and steady effect can accomplish wonders over time, so talismans are among the most effective tools magic has to offer for intentions you plan on making a permanent part of your life.

In many magical traditions, talismans take the form of disks of paper or metal with complex symbols painted, drawn, or etched on them. Most Druids who practice magic, by contrast, use a simpler approach. A short twig of a symbolically appropriate wood—one of the Ogham woods works well for this—can be marked with one or several Ogham fews, and then enchanted using any of the ritual methods covered in this chapter. Once enchanted, the talisman may be worn, tucked into a pocket, or put near a place where you spend much of your time.

If the talisman is no longer needed for some reason, and you do not want to keep its energies in place, it should be disenchanted. This is best done by a simple ritual. Open a grove in the usual way. In the Sphere of Protection, call on each of the elements to take back the energies placed in the talisman. Then, one at a time, trace the banishing form of each of the elemental symbols over the talisman, saying words such as, "O my talisman, I release you from your task. Let the energies of (element) placed in you return to their source." Imagine the elemental nwyfre flowing out of the talisman and returning to the direction of the element. When you are done, close in the usual way. The disenchanted talisman should then be washed in cold running water and left in sunlight for several hours at least. When it is thoroughly dry, it can then be burnt to release the last traces of nwyfre in it.

Two Other Enchantments

Two other forms of enchantment require a closer study and have chapters to themselves. You can apply the skills you have learned to the material thing closest to you—your own body. Work of this kind forms one of the main branches of traditional magical lore. Since the natural flows of nwyfre inside you play a crucial role in maintaining health and keeping your body alive in the first place, some care needs to be taken in bringing more nwyfre into the picture, but the Druid tradition contains proven methods to do this while increasing your health, strength, and magical power. A set of workings along these lines are covered in chapter 7.

A final and even more challenging focus for enchantment is the world around you. If the problems of today's society have their roots in the disenchantment of the world, as Max Weber suggested back in 1904, one of the greatest contributions magic can make to the present crisis is its power to reenchant the world. Like the enchantment of the body, this forms one of the main branches of traditional magical lore, and it also requires careful handling of powerful forces. A set of rituals for this purpose is given in chapter 8.

CHAPTER 7
The Secret of the Grail

Magical traditions from around the world affirm that some of the greatest secrets of magic and nature can be found within the human body itself. Like everything else in existence, the body contains nwyfre, gwyar, and calas. Its calas is the flesh and bone that give it a material form. Its gwyar is the dance of blood, lymph, and other fluids that flow through it constantly and keep it in balance. These two aspects of the body are both well understood by modern science.

The third aspect, the nwyfre of the body, has been neglected by today's materialist science but thoroughly explored in occult secret societies, as well as the healing traditions of other cultures less obsessed with materialist ideologies. Most people nowadays have heard of the chakras, seven centers of life force that play a central role in many traditions of Hindu mysticism, and the meridians, channels of life force used by Chinese healers to map out where to use massage, acupuncture, and other healing techniques. Students of Asian martial arts learn to focus their energy at the *tan t'ien* or *hara,* the point just below the navel that this system of Druid magic calls the "womb center," while practitioners of Western magical traditions have their own teachings about energy centers, such as the five centers of the Middle Pillar used in the Golden Dawn system of magic.

One thing about these systems of subtle anatomy causes confusion among many students, especially in the modern Western world: no two of them are exactly the same. Even within the same tradition, teachings vary. Hindu writings on the chakras, for example, list anything from four to twelve chakras along the spine, and those that follow the most common teaching and list seven chakras put the third one in many different places—the womb center, the solar plexus, and the region of the spleen are the most common, but other locations show up in the literature.

It's embarrassingly common for people trained in different systems to get into ferocious disputes about whose system is the right one. All such disagreements are wasted breath, because the energy centers are patterns in nwyfre—specifically in the enaid, the body of nwyfre that surrounds and penetrates our bodies of gwyar and calas—and like anything made of nwyfre, they are formed and changed by imagination and intentionality. When you are born, most of the centers in the enaid exist as potentials only, and if you never take up the challenge of a spiritual path, they remain unused potentials from cradle to grave. When you begin training in a system of spiritual development, some of those potential centers awaken, while others remain asleep. The number, nature, and position of the centers awakened by spiritual practice vary depending on the kind of inner work you do.

A complex series of tradeoffs affects the practices used in any spiritual tradition. The fewer centers you activate, the more powerful each one will be, but the fewer things you will be able to do with them; the more centers you activate, the more options you have but the weaker each will be. Centers low on the body have most of their effects in the world we experience with our physical senses; centers in the middle of the body have most of their effects in the world we experience with our thoughts, feelings, and imagination; centers in the neck and head have most of their effects on the world we experience through intuition and the spiritual senses. Depending on what you want to do with the life force, you may need a larger or smaller number of centers higher or lower on the body, and resonating with different physical organs, glands, and the like.

Many spiritual traditions use indirect methods to awaken the centers. Ordinary prayer, for example, uses a specific posture-head bowed, hands pressed palm to palm at heart level—to concentrate nwyfre at centers in the heart and throat. Sounds that resonate at specific points in the body, such as the mantras of Hindu and Buddhist traditions, have effects of the same kind.

Most of the world's traditions of ritual magic, however, awaken the centers directly, using the same tools of imagination, symbolism, and intentionality they apply to every other dimension of magical work. The exercises they use for this purpose differ just as extensively as the centers they awaken. This is as inevitable as it is appropriate, since different magical traditions have different goals, methods, symbols, sources of nwyfre, and guiding philosophies. The core exercise used in the tradition of Druid magic taught in this book, then, differs from most of the exercises you have likely encountered in other books. Its name is the Inner Grail working. It is the active working for Spirit Within, and it sums up in itself most of the work you have done so far.

The Three Cauldrons

As you have probably noticed by now, Druids like the number three, and use it fairly often to structure symbolism and ritual. The subject of the present chapter is no exception, for the Inner Grail working comprises three stages, and the first stage focuses nwyfre on three subtle centers within the enaid—three cauldrons that unite to form the Grail.

These are not the only centers of nwyfre used in Druid magic, of course, nor is the Inner Grail working the only exercise that awakens centers in the enaid. The Elemental Cross, the very first magical ritual you learned in this book, focuses nwyfre on two centers, one in the middle of the head, the other at the solar plexus. These centers are crucial in the early phases of magical training; the center in the head helps strengthen your ability to sense nwyfre, while the solar plexus is the portal through which nwyfre from outside you becomes part of your enaid.

These centers remain important, and the center in the head takes on a new role as the container for the lunar current. Two other centers of nwyfre, however—in the center of the chest and the lower belly—become crucial at this point. These centers and the one in the head have been mentioned already, in the discussion of the three currents back in chapter 1. They appear in the world's magical traditions under many different names. The names we use are the cauldrons of the earth, the Moon, and the Sun.

Before you begin working with the cauldrons in ritual, practice imagining them in your body. First, picture the cauldron of the earth in the middle of your belly, about two inches below the level of your navel. Make it four inches or so across, the color of dark bronze, with a triangle on its side to represent the secret fire. This cauldron corresponds to vitality, the passions and the material body, and forms your link with the telluric current.

Once you have this image firmly in place, picture the cauldron of the Sun in the middle of your chest at the level

Figure 7-1   The Three Cauldrons

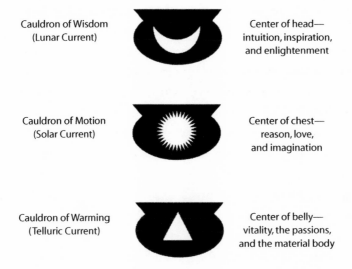

Cauldron of Wisdom
(Lunar Current)

Center of head—
intuition, inspiration,
and enlightenment

Cauldron of Motion
(Solar Current)

Center of chest—
reason, love,
and imagination

Cauldron of Warming
(Telluric Current)

Center of belly—
vitality, the passions,
and the material body

of your heart. Make it the same size as the cauldron of the earth but the color of red gold, with a sunburst on its side. It corresponds to reason, emotion, and imagination, and connects you with the solar current.

After getting this image firmly in place, picture the third cauldron, the cauldron of the Moon, in the middle of your head. Imagine it the size of the others but made of crystal, with a crescent Moon on its side. It corresponds to intuition, inspiration, and enlightenment, and forms the vessel where the lunar current will manifest once you create it.

The Three Cauldrons Ritual

When you can easily imagine all three cauldrons in their places, the next step is a ritual working to begin filling the cauldrons with nwyfre. This is best done on one of the eight holy days of the Druid calendar, but if your circumstances don't allow this, any time will do. If you have any questions

The Secret of the Grail

about your readiness for this ritual, cast an Ogham reading to settle your doubts. Set up your working space for an ordinary grove ritual, using your wand, cauldron, and crane bag, and open the grove in the usual way. When you cast the Sphere of Protection, ask the first four elements to assist you in awakening the three cauldrons inside you, and banish any obstacle that hinders you from awakening them.

Once you reach the invocations of the three forms of spirit, however, the ritual leaves familiar ground behind. When you invoke Spirit Below, trace the orange circle and say words like these: "By the bright heart of the Earth Mother, and in the great name Ced, I invoke Spirit Below, its gods, its spirits, and its powers. May a ray of the telluric current ascend into me this day and always. May the cauldron of the Moon be filled within me." Breathe in, and as you do so, imagine yourself drawing the telluric current up through the soles of both feet, up your legs, and into the lowest of the three cauldrons. As you breathe out, imagine the cauldron filled and surrounded with silvery light that ripples like water. Repeat this process, drawing the telluric current into the cauldron on the inbreath and letting it radiate there on the outbreath, nine times in all. Then say, "I thank Spirit Below for its gifts."

Go on to the invocation of Spirit Above, trace the purple circle as usual, and say words like these: "By the Sun in its glory, the father of light, and in the great name Celi, I invoke Spirit Above, its gods, its spirits, and its powers. May a ray of the solar current descend into me this day and always. May the cauldron of the Sun be filled within me." Breathe in, and as you do so, imagine yourself drawing the solar current in through your solar plexus and up to the middle cauldron at the level of your heart. As you breathe out, imagine the cauldron filled and surrounded by golden sunlight. Repeat this process, drawing the solar current into the cauldron on the inbreath and letting it radiate there on the outbreath, nine times in all. Then say, "I thank Spirit Above for its gifts."

Go on to the invocation of Spirit Within. Be aware of yourself, with the two cauldrons shining inside you and the six powers invoked and present around you. Say words like these: "By the six powers here invoked and here present, and in the grand word Awen, I invoke Spirit Within. May the lunar current be born in me this day and always. May the cauldron of the Moon be filled within me." Breathe in, and imagine silvery light rising straight up the midline of your body from the cauldron of the earth. As it reaches the cauldron of the Sun, it blends with the golden light there, and a stream of mixed silver-gold light rises the rest of the way to the cauldron of the Moon and flows into it. On the outbreath, the light in the cauldron of the Moon turns into pure white radiance, filling and surrounding the cauldron.

Repeat this process, drawing light up from the two lower cauldrons on the inbreath and converting it to white radiance on the outbreath, nine times in all. Then imagine a drop of pure white light falling from the cauldron of the Moon all the way to your solar plexus, halfway between the two lower cauldrons. Once there, it expands out in all directions to become the sphere of light used in the Circulation of Light, and you proceed as usual. Once you finish the Sphere of Protection, take your seat in the grove and meditate on the three cauldrons for a time. When you are ready, close in the usual way.

The Three Cauldrons Exercise

This ritual need be performed only once to start the process of establishing and filling the three cauldrons. Once you have done the ritual, however, regular work with the three cauldrons should become part of your daily magical practice, so that you can build on the foundations the ritual puts in place. Do the exercise as follows.

First, perform the Elemental Cross as usual, then invoke and banish the elements of air, fire, water, and earth in the usual way. When you begin the invocation of Spirit Below, trace the orange circle as usual and say words like these: "By the bright heart of the Earth Mother, and in the great name Ced, I invoke Spirit Below, its gods, its spirits, and its powers. May a ray of the telluric current ascend into me this day and always. May the cauldron of the earth be filled within me." Breathe in telluric nwyfre up through the soles of your feet and lead it into the cauldron three times. Then say, "I thank Spirit Below for its gifts."

Go on to the invocation of Spirit Above in the usual way. Trace the purple circle and say words like these: "By the Sun in its glory, the father of light, and in the great name Celi, I invoke Spirit Above, its gods, its spirits, and its powers. May a ray of the solar current descend into me this day and always. May the cauldron of the Sun be filled within me." Breathe solar nwyfre in through your solar plexus and up to the cauldron of the Sun three times, then say, "I thank Spirit Above for its gifts."

Go on next to the invocation of Spirit Within, and say words like these: "By the six powers here invoked and here present, and in the grand word Awen, I invoke Spirit Within. May the lunar current be born in me this day and always. May the cauldron of the Moon be filled within me." Breathe telluric nwyfre up from the cauldron of the earth, combine it with solar nwyfre from the cauldron of the Sun, and bring the combined currents up to fill the cauldron of the Moon three times. Then perform the circulation of light as usual.

If you find yourself in a situation where you can't perform the Sphere of Protection for some reason, an even simpler version of the Three Cauldrons exercise can be done. Simply call a ray of light down from high above you, as in the beginning of the Elemental Cross, and send it down to the center of the Earth. Then imagine the cauldron of the earth in your belly and draw telluric nwyfre into it three times with three inbreaths, as in the ritual. Imagine the cauldron of the Sun in your chest, and draw solar nwyfre into it three times with three inbreaths. Imagine the cauldron of the Moon in your head, and bring the currents up the midline of your body to it with three inbreaths. Finally, perform the circulation of light. This version should not be used often, since it lacks the balancing effect of the elemental invocations, but it works well in a pinch.

The Rising Dragons

The next phase of the Inner Grail working draws its imagery from a Celtic tradition of the Middle Ages. Two of the earliest accounts of King Arthur, the ninth-century *History of the Britons* by Nennius and the twelfth-century *History of the Kings of Britain* by Geoffrey of Monmouth, both include detailed references to it, and a different version appears in a tale in the *Mabinogion,* the story of Lludd and Llefelys.

As Nennius and Geoffrey tell it, the wicked British king Vortigern wished to build a stronghold in the mountains of northern Wales, but the stones his workmen put up each day fell down again each night. He summoned his wizards and asked them for advice, and they told him that the stronghold would stand if the blood of a child without a father was mixed into the mortar. Vortigern sent messengers throughout his kingdom, and they found a boy from the town of Caermarthen whose mother swore she had been made pregnant by no man. Nennius calls the boy Emrys, while Geoffrey gives him his more famous name: Merlin.

When Merlin came before Vortigern, however, the boy-wizard immediately took control of the situation. When he heard about the collapsing fortress and the wizards' advice, he told Vortigern to summon his wizards, and he demanded that they explain why the stronghold kept falling down. When they admitted they had no idea, Merlin told the king to have his workmen dig down beneath the building site, and predicted they would find an underground lake with two containers—vases in Nennius, hollow stones in Geoffrey—containing two serpents or dragons.

The workmen dug down and found the lake, then drained the lake and discovered the containers and the dragons just as Merlin predicted. Once uncovered, the dragons awoke and struggled against each other. At that moment, according to Geoffrey, Merlin burst into tears, entered a prophetic trance, and spoke the Prophecies of Merlin, a text as famous in the Middle Ages as the prophecies of Nostradamus are today.

R. J. Stewart, one of the most insightful modern interpreters of the Merlin legend, pointed out in his 1986 book *The Prophetic Vision of Merlin* that the rising dragons and Merlin's breakthrough into prophetic vision appear together for good reason. The dragons represent creative energies present within the land and every human being as well, and when these energies awaken and rise up through the body, they bring magical gifts of wisdom and power. This same imagery appears in the teachings of several traditional Druid orders as well, for the rising of the two dragons forms the basis of one of the most potent exercises in Druid magic.

The principle behind the exercise appears in veiled form in the old Grail legends, and can also be found written in the landscape at Glastonbury, where tradition claims the Grail had its hiding place. Two mineral springs flow near the flank of Glastonbury Tor, one flowing with red water, the other with white. These same colors appear over and over again in the Grail legends, often in the form of two lesser vessels holding the sweat and blood of Jesus, or some other pair of white and red fluids. The roses and lilies, red lions and white stags, red kings and white queens who appear so often among the symbols of alchemy point to the same thing.

It takes only a little familiarity with the language of myth to recognize that the Grail and the white and red fluids mean exactly the same thing as the underground lake and white and red dragons revealed by Merlin, or the alchemical vessel in which the red king and white queen embrace. The Grail, as we have seen, is present whenever the solar and telluric currents fuse and the lunar current is born. Yet the Grail is a vessel, a container, and the power that fills it comes from three sources. The first is the solar current, descending from above into the open mouth of the Grail in the form of the holy spear that appears alongside the sacred cup in the legend. The other two come from the land itself.

The solar and telluric currents, as mentioned back in chapter 1, give rise to two secondary currents, the red and white dragons of the legend. When these rise through the three cauldrons forming the Grail, they charge the cauldrons and strengthen them and their effects dramatically, awakening subtle perceptions and powers within the self. They also help keep the solar and telluric currents in balance within the vessel of the Grail. You can awaken the dragon currents in the same way as the three cauldrons, with a ritual working followed by a daily exercise linked to the Sphere of Protection.

The Rising Dragons Ritual

Like the Three Cauldrons ritual, the following ritual need only be done once, though the flows of nwyfre it establishes must be strengthened through regular practice of a simpler exercise afterward. It should not be performed until you have the three cauldrons solidly established in your imaginal body, a process that usually takes four to six weeks of daily practice. If you performed the Cauldron ritual on one of the eight holy days, it often works well to perform the Two Dragons ritual on the holy day following. If you have any doubts, cast an Ogham reading to settle the matter, just as though you were planning any other magical working.

Once you are ready for the working, prepare for a standard grove ritual, with wand, cauldron, and crane bag present, and open the grove in the usual way. When you invoke the four material elements, ask each element to assist you in awakening the power of the two dragons in yourself, and banish all obstacles to your success in the working. When you reach the invocations of spirit, go on as though you were doing your usual Three Cauldrons exercise, breathing nwyfre into each cauldron three times.

When you finish this stage, turn your attention to the heavens high above you. As you draw in a breath, imagine a ray of light streaming straight down from above you. It passes through the center of your head and through each of the cauldrons, and as you breathe out, it continues down to the center of the Earth. This is the holy spear, descending into the Grail to restore fertility to the land, and it also represents the rays of the Sun falling on the underground lake beneath Vortigern's tower. Repeat this same image a total of nine times, on nine breaths.

Then clasp your hands over your cauldron of Earth, an inch below your navel, and hold your elbows a little out and rounded. Make sure your knees are slightly bent and your weight rests equally on both feet. These details of posture help guide the currents through your enaid and physical body along the proper paths.

Next, turn your attention to the earth below your feet. Reach deep into the Earth with your imagination, and picture the heart of the Earth ablaze with light. From that deep source of light, imagine two currents of nwyfre rising up, one red and one white, like twin serpents or dragons. The red one rises until its head is just below the sole of your right foot, and the white to just below the sole of your left foot.

Next, bring the red current up through your right leg and the white current through your left leg, and draw them into your cauldron of the earth. The two currents cross there, so that the white current flows to your right side and the red to your left. They flow into your arms, curve out and then back in, and flow into your cauldron of the Sun. Here they cross again, so that the red is again on the right and the white on the left. The two currents arc up the sides of your head and neck and flow into your cauldron of the Moon. Here they fuse in a blaze of pure light, as shown in Figure 7-2.

Repeat this upward motion of the two currents nine times in all. It often works best to take two breaths in the course of each upward movement—breathing in as the currents flow up your legs to the cauldron of the earth; out as

Figure 7-2 The Two Dragon Currents

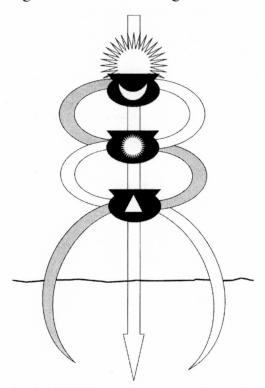

they flow out and back inwards to the cauldron of the Sun; in again as they flow out and back inwards to the cauldron of the Moon; out again as they fuse and fill the cauldron of the Moon with blinding light. If you need to take more breaths, however, by all means do so. The goal of the ritual is to get the imagery and flow of the rising dragons firmly established, not to get it done quickly.

When the dragons have risen to your cauldron of the Moon nine times, go on to the Circulation of Light as usual. Take your seat in the grove, and meditate on the two dragons, then close. If you feel dizzy, as many people do after this ritual, eat something to bring yourself back down to the material world.

The Rising Dragons Exercise

Once you perform the Rising Dragons ritual as described, a simpler working can be used to build on the foundations established by the ritual. The exercise expands further on the Sphere of Protection, and is done as follows.

Begin as usual with the Elemental Cross, and invoke and banish the elements of air, fire, water, and earth in the standard way. Then invoke the elements of Spirit Below, Spirit Above, and Spirit Within to fill the three cauldrons, just as you did in the Three Cauldrons exercise.

Next, as in the ritual, imagine a ray of the solar current descending from infinitely far above you, passing through the three cauldrons and into the center of the Earth beneath you. Repeat this image three times in all.

Then clasp your hands over your cauldron of Earth, and imagine the dragon currents rising from the heart of the Earth to the soles of your feet. Bring them spiraling up through your body, using the same breathing pattern as in the ritual. Do this three times in all, and then perform the Circulation of Light as usual.

If you find yourself in a situation where you can't perform the Sphere of Protection for some reason, an even simpler version of the Rising Dragons exercise can be done. Simply call a ray of light down from high above you, as in the beginning of the Elemental Cross, and send it down to the center of the Earth. Next, establish the three cauldrons in the usual way and breathe nwyfre into each cauldron three times. After that, imagine the descending spear of light three times, and then bring the dragon currents up three times in the way just outlined, and finish with the Circulation of Light. As with the simplified Three Cauldrons exercise, this shouldn't be done too often because it lacks the balance of the material elements, but it works well when waving your arms around isn't an option.

The Tree of Light

The third and final phase of the Inner Grail working unfolds from a symbolism found all over the world. Many traditional mythologies picture the world as a mighty tree with its roots in the underworld, its branches holding the worlds in place, and its crown reaching up to the highest realms of spirit. It's a powerful image and, like all myths, it can be understood on many different levels. It has obvious relevance to Druid magic, because trees draw their life from above and below at the same time—their roots bring up minerals and water from deep within the Earth, while their leaves soak up sunlight and carbon dioxide from the heavens—just as Druid magic draws power from both the solar and telluric currents (see Figure 7-3).

The image of the world tree also has potent links to the lore of spiritual transformation. Countless myths of the attainment of wisdom include the world tree as a central feature. The Norse wizard god Odin hanging on the world tree Yggdrasil for nine nights to win the secret of the runes, and Gautama the Buddha achieving nirvana while seated at the foot of the Bo tree, are two examples. Another example, though it's not often recognized as one, is the crucifixion of Jesus. The *Gospel of Truth,* one of the Gnostic gospels, says of Jesus: "He was nailed to a tree and he became a fruit of the knowledge [gnosis] of the Father" (Robinson, 1988, p. 41).

Figure 7-3 The World Tree

Many Gnostics, as this text shows, believed that Jesus brought *gnosis*—the spiritual knowledge that transforms the self—to humankind through his crucifixion. Like Odin, the Buddha, and many other mythic figures, his self-surrender in the presence of a tree won the gift of knowledge. The Gnostics were not the only ones who pictured the cross as a living tree, either—many medieval images of Jesus' crucifixion show the same unexpected image.

Like every other mythic image, this conjunction of the tree, the holy person, and the gift of wisdom has many meanings and lessons. The simple fact that sitting with your back against a tree very often helps deepen your meditations is not the least of them! Still, another meaning in this combination of symbols has an important secret to teach the Druid mage.

Some of the most insightful studies of tree symbolism, such as E. A. S Butterworth's *The Tree at the Navel of the Earth,* suggest that these myths of revelation at the world tree relate to one of the hidden potentials of the human enaid. Many people nowadays have heard of kundalini yoga, the art of rousing the "serpent power" at the base of the spine and leading it up to the crown of the head. This is one expression of a widely known magical technique—the opening of a central channel of nwyfre along the midline of the body.

Different magical and mystical systems use this channel in many ways. Kundalini yoga opens the channel to bring energy up from below and awaken the seven chakras. The Golden Dawn's Middle Pillar exercise, by contrast, brings nwyfre down the central channel from above, and uses it to awaken five energy centers. The difference in technique comes from the fact that these two systems don't draw nwyfre from the same sources or work toward the same goals. Each one does what it needs to do to reach the goals it sets itself. The same can be said for the countless other traditions that use the central channel to direct nwyfre. In Druid magic, as you've probably guessed already, the central channel opens to a twofold flow of nwyfre from the macrocosm—upward from the telluric current and downward from the solar current.

The process of opening the central channel actually began with the very first gesture of the Sphere of Protection, the first ritual you learned in this book, when you brought down a ray of light from far above and sent it down into the depths of the Earth. All the invocations of Spirit Above and Below and the work with the solar and telluric currents took the process further, and the first two stages of the Inner Grail working brought it to a new level by establishing centers of nwyfre along your body's centerline, and bringing the two dragon currents into play to balance and sustain the central channel.

The third stage of the Inner Grail working completes the sequence by formulating the central channel anew and opening it to the nwyfre of the macrocosm. As with the first two stages, an initial ritual to establish the imagery needs to be followed by regular practice with a simpler exercise. As you work through these stages, the central channel will open slowly and naturally. Methods of opening the central channel in a hurry do exist, but these need to be learned under the close supervision of an experienced teacher, and involve substantial risks to your physical and mental health. A more patient approach gets the same results, and can be followed successfully from written instructions like these.

The Tree of Light Ritual

Like the rituals that began the first two phases of the Grail working, the following ritual need only be done once, though regular practice is just as important once you perform it. Before you attempt it, be sure you have the two dragon currents well established in your imaginal body, a process that usually takes four to six weeks of daily practice. If you performed the Rising Dragons Ritual on one of the eight holy days, it often works well to perform the Tree of Light ritual on the holy day following. As before, cast an Ogham reading to be sure you are ready.

Prepare for a standard grove ritual, with wand, cauldron, and crane bag present, and open the grove in the usual way. When you invoke the four material elements, ask each element to assist you in bringing the Tree of Light into being in yourself, and banish all obstacles to your success in the working. When you reach the invocations of spirit, go on as though you were doing your usual Three Cauldrons and Rising Dragons exercises, breathing nwyfre into each cauldron three times, and then bringing the dragon currents up through the cauldrons three times.

At this point in the working, imagine a point of light descending from your cauldron of the Moon to your solar plexus center, as though you were about to begin the Circulation of Light. Instead of expanding it into a sphere, though, hold it at your solar plexus center for a time, imagining it as a seed. Let the seed of light sprout, sending a slender stem of light upward and a root of light downward. Watch it grow into a sapling, and then into a tree, putting out branches and leaves of light above you and roots of light below. Feel sunlight and wind on the leaves, soil and water around the roots, the firmness of the trunk connecting them. Spend as much time as you need to make the image of the tree as clear and solid as possible.

Next, turn your attention to your breath. As you breathe in, imagine the leaves drawing in air, sunlight, and the nwyfre of the solar current, and sending them down through the trunk all the way to the deepest root. As you breathe out, imagine the roots drawing in water, nutrients from the soil, and the nwyfre of the telluric current, and sending them through the trunk all the way to the highest leaf. Repeat this nine times in all.

Finally, turn your attention back to your solar plexus, and imagine that the seed of light is still there, in the heart of the Tree of Light. Expand it into a sphere as usual, making the sphere large enough to surround the entire Tree of Light, and then perform the Circulation of Light as you usually do. Take your seat in the grove and meditate on the image of the Tree of Light. When you are ready, close the grove in the ordinary way.

The Tree of Light Exercise

The Tree of Light exercise builds on your previous daily ritual practices—the Sphere of Protection, Three Cauldrons exercise, and Rising Dragons exercise—and includes all of these. Plan on practicing it regularly from the time you perform the Tree of Light ritual, for as long as you choose to follow the path of Druid magic.

Begin by performing the Elemental Cross as usual, and invoke and banish the elements of air, fire, water, and earth in the standard way. Next, invoke the elements of Spirit Below, Spirit Above, and Spirit Within to fill the three cauldrons, just as you did in the Three Cauldrons exercise. Bring the ray of solar light down from above to the center of the Earth, summon the two dragon currents and bring them up through your body and the three cauldrons, just as you did in the Rising Dragons exercise.

Then, let a seed of light descend from your cauldron of wisdom to your solar plexus center, and imagine the Tree of Light growing from that seed until it extends far above and below you. Once the tree is established, bring the solar current down to the roots on each inbreath, and bring the telluric current up to the leaves on each outbreath. Repeat this three times in all. Finish by performing the Circulation of Light as usual.

Regular practice of this exercise, once you have worked your way through the rituals and exercises leading up to it, will open door after door to your magical and spiritual advancement. As your practice ripens, so will your ability to sense and shape nwyfre and work magic in yourself and the world around you. This ripening process will bring you to an inescapable challenge. Now that you hold the keys to magical power, what will you do with them?

PART THREE
The Way of Druid Magic

CHAPTER 8
The Reenchantment of the World

The question of the purposes of magic becomes more and more necessary to confront as you progress further in magic. As with all things magical, different people and traditions answer it differently. To some, magic is a practical craft, and its purpose is to make life happier and better for the mage and his or her family, friends, and clients. To others, magic is a path of service, and its purpose is to serve the community, the gods, or the living Earth. To still others, magic is a way of mystical transformation, and its purpose is to lift the mage above the ordinary limitations of humanity—in the words of the old Druid lore, to pass from Abred, the world of limitation and mortality, into Gwynfydd, the realm of freedom and conscious immortality.

Many of the traditions that affirm one of these goals condemn the others for one reason or another. The Druid tradition, as you have probably guessed by now, takes a different tack. From a Druid perspective, all of these are valid purposes, and one of the tasks you face is the discovery of whatever blending of these purposes fulfills your own deepest needs. You may find yourself called to one of the three alone, or to a combination of two of them, or to some fusion of all three. Since each created being is unique, and fills a unique niche in the great pattern of all things, no one rule will work for all.

The techniques and tools of Druid magic that you have learned in this book can be used for any of these purposes, or all of them. You are also free to draw on lore from other magical traditions as you create your own personal approach to Druid magic, and you will find that magic from many other systems can be integrated with the methods taught in this book. Most of the possible purposes of magical work have been covered at great length in recent magical literature.

One of the central themes of modern Druid magic, however, rarely appears in other occult books. This theme unfolds from points made in the first chapter of this book. When Max Weber spoke more than a century ago of the disenchantment of the world, he pointed to one of the greatest needs of the present age of the world. If the modern industrial world is literally disenchanted—suffering from a shortage of enchantment, a loss of the magic that once wove humanity and nature together into a single fabric—then one of the crucial tasks of mages today is nothing less than the reenchantment of the world.

Enchantment, as you learned in chapter 1, is the art of awakening spiritual forces in material things. Before the dawn of industrial society, and even today in cultures where modern materialist ways of thought have not shouldered aside older and wiser ways of relating to the living world, enchantment was and is part of everyday reality. Enchantment played an essential role in balancing the rights of the individual with the needs of the community, keeping human actions within ecological limits, and weaving humanity and nature together into a single fabric.

It's popular nowadays, especially among apologists for modern industrial culture, to speak of these enchantments as "superstitions" or "taboos," but such terms conceal both the power of the old enchantments of nature and their ecological relevance. All over the world, traditional enchantments protected sacred groves from the axe, made certain areas off limits to farming, herding, or hunting, and kept other interactions between humanity and nature within precise limits. Time and again, when ecologists have studied these old "superstitions," they have been astonished to find solid environmental common sense underlying them—sacred groves commonly grow in the right spots to prevent soil erosion, animal species forbidden to hunters turn out to harbor dangerous diseases, and so on.

Those modern scholars who notice the ecological realities behind these enchantments very often claim that their magical dimension is either a symbolic way of talking about wholly material phenomena, or a way of tricking people into behaving the way they should. Magical philosophy suggests another alternative. The enchanted world of traditional societies establishes an intentionality that helps make people aware of their place in a larger community, rewards those who walk in harmony with nature, and corrects those who refuse to do so. The loss of the old enchantments thus does much to explain the blind arrogance that drives modern industrial society from one preventable ecological disaster to another.

According to magical lore, however, the web of enchantments that unites humanity with the land has effects on non-human nature as well. Human cooperation with the cycles of nature, old traditions teach, brings balance and fertility to the natural world. This makes perfect sense in magical terms. Since nwyfre follows intentionality, an intentionality that brings human beings and nature into balance has positive results all through the ecosystem on every level. Just as ignorant and arrogant human actions can create wastelands out of forests, human actions guided by wisdom and a clear sense of ecological reality can not only turn wastelands back into thriving ecosystems but help nature flourish even more abundantly than she does on her own.

Enchantments so potent take centuries to establish, and—at least according to tradition—also need the conscious cooperation of other beings, ranging from animals and plants through nature spirits to the great powers of the cosmos that human beings call gods and goddesses. Even a lifetime spent in Druid magic can only begin the process of restoring the ancient web of enchantment. Still, no other application of the art of magic has so much relevance to the needs of today as the work of reawakening the enchantments of the Grail and healing today's Waste Land. The ritual workings explored in this chapter provide several ways to begin work on this great and profoundly necessary task.

Cleansing the Land

One of the most heartbreaking results of our society's blindness to its own roots in the living world is the casual devastation inflicted on so many natural environments. Three centuries into the Industrial Age, few corners of the Earth have escaped damage from the discarded poisons, resource extraction, and sheer careless waste of a civilization that imagines it will not have to live with the consequences of its mistreatment of its planetary home. Plenty of hard work of every kind, from tree planting and erosion control to changes in attitudes, will be needed to repair the damage and stop any more from occurring.

Magic has a role to play, however, because patterns in the nwyfre can shape human and nonhuman actions alike, speeding the healing of the land while it helps shelter recovering ecosystems from further damage. By the time you begin exploring the rituals in this chapter, if you have worked your way through the earlier sections of this book, you know that magic can have remarkable effects on your own life, even in its most practical dimensions. Magic can do the same thing for natural ecosystems. It cannot substitute for other forms of work, but it can do things no other kind of work can do. It can catalyze subtle changes in the Earth that can literally speed up the breakdown of toxins in the soil and water, as well as banishing the subtler toxins of ignorance, selfishness, and greed that put the more material pollutants there in the first place.

The choice of a place to cleanse is of some importance. The influence of the media leads many people to think of nature as something that only matters in wilderness areas and national parks, and so many people who want to use magic to help the natural world focus on a handful of famous places and neglect opportunities much closer to home. Nature is a complex web, however, and many times the places that most need cleansing and healing lie scarcely noticed on the fringes of industrial society: a vacant lot overgrown with weeds where local birds nest, a neglected marsh critical for the spawning cycles of a rare species of fish, a patch of woodland where animals find homes among abandoned cars and decades-old junk. Such places form what ecologists call *refugia,* small patches of living nature from which recovery can take place as the ravages of industrial civilization draw to an end, and they call for at least as much care and healing as more famous and photogenic places far away.

Another cautionary note belongs here. Many people in the modern alternative spirituality movement, seeing the dilapidated state of many ancient sacred sites, decide that the best starting point for the reenchantment of the world is the nearest holy place they can find. It is hard to think of a less constructive notion. Many places made sacred by the ancients still possess a magic far subtler and stronger than anything in the fragmentary occult teachings that are all we have to work with today. Trying to repair a holy place on the basis of the material in this book is a little like trying to perform brain surgery using a first-aid textbook as your guide.

This is especially true in regions such as North America and Australia, where the people who built the sacred sites have been driven off their lands and confined to reservations by European invaders in recent centuries. Many of the old holy places are still visited and tended secretly by descendants of the original builders, and ignorant magical work done with no understanding of native traditions can do much more harm than good. Unless you have been invited to help cleanse a sacred site by a native elder who has the right to make that invitation, then you have no business imposing your magic in such a place.

As a general rule, the closer to home you start your personal contribution to the reenchantment of the world, the more constructive good you will do. As you learn to notice your own environment, you will find that there is no shortage of places that need to be cleansed and blessed. Many Druids find that their own backyards are a good starting place for this work, and local spots where nature keeps a foothold make a good next step. Such steps may seem modest at first glance, but when you wake to the sound of native birdsong for the first time in years, or watch wildflowers burst into life in what had been a patch of invasive weeds, you will see that the results are well worth the effort.

The following ritual is one of many possible ways to use magic to cleanse land and heal the damage done to it by human neglect and mismanagement. Experiment with it, and then create your own rituals for the same purpose.

A Land-Cleansing Ritual

Before you begin ritual work, all the usual preliminaries need to be done first. Meditate on your intention and cast an Ogham divination to be sure your intention is appropriate. It can also be wise to use scrying to explore the options before beginning ritual work; simply use a mental image of the place itself as a doorway for scrying, and ask to speak to the spirits of the place. Tell them what you have in mind, and ask them if they approve. If they do, ask them if they have any requests or advice concerning the ritual, and act accordingly if they do. You will find that the information you get in this way can increase the positive effects of this work in dramatic ways.

This ritual is best done in the open air, standing on the piece of land you seek to cleanse and bless. If circumstances make this impossible, do the ritual in a private place as close as possible to the place to be cleansed. In this latter case, take a stone or a small handful of earth from the place to be cleansed, and put it in the center of the altar before you begin. You will also need the four cauldrons for incense, flame, water, and earth, as well as your wand. Open the grove with the cauldrons in the usual way.

When you perform the Sphere of Protection, call on the elements to bless the land with their power, and take away any pollution or damage from the land. When you finish the opening and take your seat, use green color breathing to prepare for the meditation, and then meditate on the idea of cleansing and purifying the land.

When you are ready, rise and approach the altar. Say words like these: "I invoke the power of Ced, the Earth Mother to heal and bless this land. Let all pollution depart from it and all damage be healed. Let it and all the living things that depend on it be restored to radiant health." If you cannot perform the ritual on the land itself, change the wording of this and all other parts of the ritual to refer to the land you intend to cleanse, rather than the place where you are performing the working.

Circle around to the east side of the altar, facing the center, and say, "Let the powers of air arise and cleanse this place." Pick up the cauldron of incense, take it to the eastern edge of the place, and raise it high in both hands. Say words like these: "In the name of Hu and by the powers of the realm of air I cleanse this land and call the powers of healing to it." Concentrate on the idea that the incense smoke is summoning cleansing winds to bring healing to the land. When it feels right, return the cauldron to the altar.

Circle around to the south side of the altar, facing the center, and say: "Let the powers of fire arise and cleans this place." Pick up the fire cauldron, take it to the southern edge of the place, and raise it high in both hands. Say words like these: "In the name of Sul and by the powers of the realm of fire I cleanse this land and call the powers of healing to it." Concentrate on the idea that the heat of the flame is summoning cleansing sunlight and warmth to bring healing to the land. When it feels right, return the cauldron to the center of the altar.

Circle around to the west side of the altar, facing the center, and say, "Let the powers of water arise and cleanse this place." Pick up the water cauldron, take it to the western edge of the place, and raise it high in both hands. Say words like these: "In the name of Esus and by the powers of the realm of water I cleanse this land and call the powers of healing to it." Concentrate on the idea that the water is summoning cleansing rains and flowing water to bring healing to the land. When it feels right, return the cauldron to the center of the altar.

Circle around to the north side of the altar, facing the center, and say, "Let the powers of earth arise and cleanse this place." Pick up the earth cauldron, take it to the northern edge of the place, and raise it high in both hands. Say words like these: "In the name of Elen and by the powers of the realm of earth I cleanse this land and call the powers of healing to it." Concentrate on the idea that the salt or earth is summoning chemical processes in the earth to bring healing to the land. When it feels right, return the cauldron to the center of the altar.

Turn your attention to the land beneath you, and imagine the telluric current rising up from the heart of the Earth. Say words like these: "When the four material elements are in balance, the element of spirit appears in their midst." Pick up the wand, and use it to trace an invoking heather pentagram over the altar, saying, "I invoke Spirit Below. Let the telluric current arise and bless this land." Imagine silver light rising up from the center of the Earth to fill the land and every living thing on, in, and above it with vitality and health. Make this image as vivid as possible, and maintain it for at least several minutes before releasing it.

Release the image, then turn your attention to the sky above you. Imagine the solar current cascading down through space from the Sun. Pick up the wand and use it to trace an invoking oak pentagram over the altar, saying words like these: "I invoke Spirit Above. Let the solar current descend and bless this land." Imagine golden light descending from the skies to fill the land and every living thing on, in, and above it with vitality and health. Make this image as vivid as possible, and maintain it for several minutes at least.

Hold the wand vertically with both hands above the altar, in the middle of the space where you traced the two pentagrams. Say words like these: "From above to below, from below to above, the two currents are awakened. I invoke Spirit Within. Let the lunar current be born within this land and fill it with the power of Awen." Imagine the golden solar current and the silver telluric current both shining into the land at once, and then see them fuse into pure white light, the color of lightning. Imagine the disk of the Moon surrounding the land and everything in it. Once again, make this image as vivid as possible, and hold it for several minutes at least.

Once this is done, close the grove in the usual way. If you have done the working somewhere other than the place you intend to cleanse and bless, take the stone or earth that has been at the center of the altar and return it to the place where the effects of the working are meant to focus. The material link will help anchor the energies to the proper place.

As with any working, the best way to anchor the effects of the magic in the material world is to do something practical to further your intention. For this type of working, you might choose to get sturdy gloves and a trash bag or two, and pick up all the litter you can find on the piece of land you have worked magic to heal. If circumstances make this sort of direct action impossible, a change in your own life to significantly reduce the burden your lifestyle places on the living Earth will have the same positive effects.

Restoring Fertility to the Land

One of the classic purposes for magical ritual is to bring fertility to the land, and this is even more necessary today than it once was. Once the basic work of cleaning and healing has been done, the restoration of natural fertility forms a second vital step, and magic can accomplish this at a level of subtlety and power no other human action can manage.

In ancient times, when wild ecosystems thrived in balance with their surroundings and human beings were still struggling to master the subtle magic of agriculture, most such rituals aimed at bringing fertility to the fields and gardens on which human life depended. Nowadays, by contrast, it is difficult to find any place on the Earth's surface that has not been affected by human mismanagement, and magical workings to restore fertility are needed just as much in the wilderness as in places harmed by industrial agriculture or ecologically ignorant landscaping.

In magical terms, fertility comes into being from the fusion of the solar and telluric currents. When land becomes barren, the contact between the two currents has become blocked and needs to be reestablished. The traditions of Druid magic offer several different ways to restore the free flow of the two currents.

Perhaps the simplest and most inconspicuous way to do this draws on the ritual work you have already learned. The

Inner Grail working, like any magical working, sets up momentum in the nwyfre in the place where it is performed. Since it draws on the solar and telluric currents and creates the lunar current from them, it fosters the fusion of the currents in nature. When circumstances don't allow you to do ritual work openly, simply sit or stand in the area you intend to affect and do the simplest version of the complete Inner Grail exercise given in chapter 7, including the Three Cauldrons, the Dragon Currents, and the World Tree. Repeat this as often as you can, concentrating on the idea that this working brings fertility to the land.

Another simple and effective way to restore fertility to an area is to plant a tree, and water and tend the sapling until it can grow by itself. Trees have important magical and energetic properties over and above their contributions to the material side of an ecosystem. The vertical line of the trunk becomes a channel through which solar and telluric currents flow and interact. *The Druidry Handbook* includes information on planting trees and a simple ritual for blessing a newly planted tree, and these can be valuable resources for any effort to restore fertility to a place where it has become blocked.

Where circumstances permit, however, a stronger magic with deep roots in Druid tradition can be put to use. This begins with setting up a standing stone in the affected area to serve as a channel for the two currents and a vessel for the creation of the lunar current. The stone need not be large—I have seen good results come from a stone only 18 inches tall—but it should be no more than half as wide as it is tall, and needs to be natural stone; concrete or other artificial substances are worse than useless. A third of the stone's length should be underground, and two thirds above, as shown in Figure 8-1.

Figure 8-1   The Standing Stone

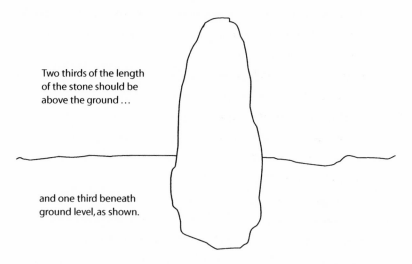

Two thirds of the length of the stone should be above the ground …

and one third beneath ground level, as shown.

Once the stone is in place, it will begin forming a connection between the solar and telluric currents all by itself. You can make this process work more swiftly and powerfully with magical ritual. The following ritual shows one way this can be done, using the formula of the Inner Grail working. Experiment with it, learn its lessons, and then devise your own rituals for the same purpose.

A Standing Stone Working

This working is best done between Imbolc and Alban Heruin, to take advantage of the rising strength of the solar current. For best results, schedule it on a morning between dawn and noon, on a day when the Moon is waxing. As with any working, you should meditate on your intention and cast an Ogham reading beforehand to be sure your plans are appropriate, and scrying is also a valuable tool for this work.

Set up the space for an ordinary grove ritual, with the four cauldrons of the elements placed around the stone as though on an altar, and a chair in the north. Open the grove in the usual way, using the cauldrons in place of your wand. When you purify the space with the four elements and bring each cauldron back to the center, purify the stone as well by making a circle around it with each element. When you cast the Sphere of Protection, ask the four material elements to help you bring fertility to the land, and banish everything that hinders fertility there.

When you reach the invocations of the three forms of spirit, the distinctive phase of this ritual begins. When you invoke Spirit Below, trace the orange circle over the stone and say words like these: "By the bright heart of the Earth Mother, and in the great name Ced, I invoke Spirit Below, its gods, its spirits, and its powers. May a ray of the telluric current ascend into this stone now and always." Imagine the telluric current rising up from the depths of the Earth into the stone, filling it with silvery light that ripples like water. Concentrate on this for several minutes at least. Then say, "I thank Spirit Below for its gifts."

Go on to the invocation of Spirit Above, trace the purple circle in the air above the stone, and say words like these: "By the Sun in its glory, the father of light, and in the great name Celi, I invoke Spirit Above, its gods, its spirits, and its powers. May a ray of the solar current descend into this stone now and always." Imagine the solar current descending from the sky into the stone, filling it with golden sunlight. Concentrate on this for several minutes at least. Then say, "I thank Spirit Above for its gifts."

Go on to the invocation of Spirit Within. Say words like these: "By the six powers here invoked and here present, and in the grand word *Awen,* I invoke Spirit Within. May the lunar current be born in this stone now and always." Imagine the silver and gold nwyfre within the stone fusing into pure white radiance and radiating outward into the ground. Concentrate on this for several minutes at least.

When you finish this stage, turn your attention to the heavens high above you. Imagine a ray of light streaming straight down from above the stone, passing through it and descending down to the center of the Earth. This brings the solar current through the stone to heal any imbalances in the nwyfre of the land. Concentrate on this image for several minutes at least.

Next, turn your attention to the earth below your feet. Reach deep into the Earth with your imagination, and picture the heart of the Earth ablaze with light. From that deep source of light, imagine two currents of nwyfre rising up, one red and one white, like twin serpents or dragons. The red one is to your right, the white one to your left. The two currents cross just below the stone, then again at the midpoint of the stone, and finally unite just above the stone in a blaze of pure light. Again, concentrate on this image for several minutes at least.

Next, imagine a point of light in the heart of the stone, where the two dragon currents cross. Imagine it as a seed. Let the seed of light sprout, sending a slender stem of light upward and a root of light downward. Watch it grow into a sapling, and then into a tree, putting out branches and leaves of light above the stone and roots of light below. Feel sunlight and wind on the leaves, soil and water around the roots, the firmness of the trunk connecting them. Spend as much time as you need to make the image of the tree as clear and solid as possible.

Next, imagine the leaves drawing in air, sunlight, and the nwyfre of the solar current, and sending them down through the trunk all the way to the deepest root. Imagine the roots drawing in water, nutrients from the soil, and the nwyfre of the telluric current, and sending them through the trunk all the way to the highest leaf. This is the most important phase of the working, and you should concentrate on it for several minutes at least, with as much intensity as you can.

Finally, turn your attention back to the stone. Imagine a sphere of light expanding outward from the stone until it encloses the entire area you wish to bless with fertility. Perform the Circulation of Light as you usually do. Take your seat in the grove and meditate on the image of the Tree of Light. When you are ready, close the grove in the ordinary way.

This working may be repeated once a year to increase its effect, preferably on the same date you originally performed it. Repeated annual workings set up a rhythm in the nwyfre that can yield spectacular results.

Consecrating Sacred Spaces

One further dimension of the Earth magic introduced in this chapter deserves discussion here. While it is inappropriate for anyone but experts and traditional elders to attempt intensive magical work with ancient holy sites, nothing prevents even a novice at Druid magic from creating a new sacred place and working with its energies. Since the power of the place will depend on your own skills as an enchanter, you can be sure you will not get in over your depth, and as your skills increase, so will the powers of the place you have enchanted.

A deeper issue also makes this a worthwhile option. In our disenchanted world, sacred spaces are few and far between, while cultures that embrace the art of enchantment and the holiness of nature usually create holy places all over the landscape. It is precisely at sacred places, where spiritual forces flow freely through the veils of matter, that the enchantments that once held the world in balance can most easily be rewoven; it is at sacred places where people can communicate most easily with the spiritual powers in nature, and where the blessings of the gods and goddesses flow most easily into the world.

Even the humblest and simplest of sacred places can have such effects. All over Japan today, for example, shrines dedicated to the indigenous Japanese nature religion, Shinto, can be found. Some of them are major religious sites with full-time priests and priestesses, but many others are tiny precincts tucked in among houses or fields, visited by a traveling priest once a year, or stones set up along roadsides and marked only by a bit of carving and a few offerings. All of them, the simple stones as well as the great centers, provide contact points between people and the *kami,* the spiritual powers revered by Shinto. The same thing can be found all over the world where the living traditions of nature-centered spirituality have not been obliterated by the irrational "rationality" of industrial culture.

Certain practical issues have to be considered in any attempt to build sacred sites of the same kind here and now. The most important is that once you enchant a sacred place, it stays enchanted. According to some magical traditions, the consecration of a holy place lasts for 2,160 years, or one of the twelve astrological months of the Great Year, so you need to plan ahead! For this reason among others, you should be more than usually careful to be sure your intention is appropriate before beginning the work. Meditation and divination both have their places in this process, but much can be learned by simply sitting quietly in the place you hope to enchant, day after day, trying to feel the character of the space. Ask the land if it wishes to become a sacred place, and listen for the answer.

Traditionally each sacred place is under the guardianship of a god or goddess, and making contact with the deity of the place also forms part of the preliminary work. Whatever spiritual practices you find most useful should be put to work here. You may choose a deity for the place and then seek the deity's permission to dedicate the place to his or her worship, or you may simply find a place that seeks enchantment and then open yourself to whatever god or goddess desires to manifest there. Both approaches are traditional and effective, and whichever one fits your needs and the religious traditions you follow may be used. Since this dimension of the work belongs to religion rather than magic, however, no more will be said about it here.

The rituals you use to enchant your sacred space will similarly depend on the religious traditions you follow and the deity you intend to invoke. The magical side of the work may be done using any of the rituals for enchantment presented in this book, or by way of an original ritual designed to fit the details of the space and the purposes of the working. It often works well to open a grove in the usual way, perform the magical side of the enchantment, then invoke the god or goddess using whatever religious methods you prefer, and close in the usual way after a time for meditation and reflection. Once you enchant your holy place, whatever rituals you plan on doing there should begin as soon as possible thereafter, but this again will depend on the work you have in mind and the preferences of the deity you invoke.

A sacred space may also be enchanted through a series of workings. This works particularly well if you plan on making that classic Druid sacred space, a stone circle. One very effective approach starts by selecting eight stones for the circle plus a ninth for the central altar. On one of the Druid holy days, erect the stone corresponding to that day, and enchant it using the standing stone ritual already given in this chapter. On the next holy day, erect and enchant the next stone, and so on around the wheel of the year. On the anniversary of your placing the first stone, put in the altar stone, and at that time invoke the deity who will be the guardian of your stone circle. The result will be a powerful ritual and spiritual space. On the other hand, you can erect all the stones at once and enchant them one at a time as circumstances permit, and then use rituals performed regularly in your stone circle to finish the process of enchanting and empowering the place.

Beyond these few guidelines, you will need to work out your own approach to the art of crafting sacred space. If you have worked your way through the rituals and exercises in this book, you will have more than enough skill and experience to build and enchant a sacred space suited to your needs and those of the spiritual powers you wish to invoke. As industrial society moves further into its inevitable collision with ecological reality, skills and experience of this kind offer some of the few positive ways to bring humanity back into harmony with the living earth and begin the process of healing the damage that our species has caused over the last few centuries. What part you choose to play in that great work of Druid magic is up to you, for the Druid path offers no simple answers, and each of us who walks that path does so in a different way. May your journey bring joy to you and blessing to the Earth!

APPENDIX
Deities in Welsh Druid Traditions

While many books currently available discuss the old Irish pantheon, most accounts of the deities revered by Welsh and English Druids in the nineteenth and early twentieth centuries are long out of print. Since these gods and goddesses are central to the Druid Revival tradition and play a major role in Druid magic, an account of them may be useful to Druids interested in the magical as well as the religious dimensions of Druidry.

It probably needs to be said that no solid evidence ties most of these divinities or their worship back to the ancient Celtic Druids. Modern Druidry traces its roots back only as far as the eighteenth century; the Druid movement in Wales, though it drew substantially on surviving fragments of medieval Welsh lore, also relied, like every other living spiritual tradition, on its own experiences and insights. Still, historical authenticity is as irrelevant in matters of religion as it is in magic. The consensus of many hundreds of modern Druids is that the gods and goddesses of the Welsh Druid tradition respond when they are invoked, and this is ultimately the only thing that matters.

Many Neopagan traditions nowadays consider the members of the three great families of Welsh myth—the Plant Don, Plant Annwn, and Plant Llyr—to be gods and goddesses. In the traditions discussed here, however, these beings belong to a second order, superhuman but less mighty than the gods, and subject to time and fate. Students of Platonism, a philosophy much studied by nineteenth century Druids, may recall the difference Plato notes in the *Timaeus* between the eternal gods and the created gods; a similar concept seems to have shaped the theology of the Druid Revival.

Ana

The goddess of the planet Earth itself, as distinct from its biosphere, Ana is the mother of Ced and the grandmother of most of the other gods and goddesses; she rules the deep places of the Earth. Imagine her as an ancient woman with long white hair, dressed in dark robes of archaic design, with a long staff in her hands and ornate rings on her fingers.

Beli

The year god who dies and is reborn at the winter solstice, Beli traces out the cycle of the seasons as he passes through the stages of his journey from pale infant to strong young god, to lover and mate of the living Earth, to king, to sacrifice, to pale corpse laid out on the bier of the sky. Imagine him at any of these stages, or more generally as a strong and virile man with golden hair and beard, wearing a red tunic and cloak ornamented with gold, and carrying a long spear and a golden shield.

Belinus

Another name of Beli, chosen because its seven letters in their Greek form, βηλενδζ, add to 365—the number of days in a year—in Greek gematria.

Ced

The goddess of the Earth's biosphere, Ced is the primary female expression of the divine in Welsh Druid lore. Her name means "bounty" or "assistance" in Welsh. She is the spouse and equal of Celi the sky god, and also by turns the mother, mate, and layer-out of Belinus at the various stages of his yearly journey. Imagine her as a beautiful mature woman with long flowing brown hair, wearing a green gown and a cloak made of every kind of leaves.

Celi

The god of infinite space, Celi is the primary male expression of the divine in Welsh Druid lore. His name means "heaven," and he is also called Hen Ddihenydd, the Ancient of Days. According to Welsh Druid tradition he is hidden from human sight and only reveals himself as pure light. Imagine him in the form of the three rays of light, / | \ , streaming down from the heavens onto the Earth.

Ceridwen

The goddess of the Moon, Ceridwen—the name means "bent woman," and refers to the shape Americans call "the man in the Moon" and Welsh tradition pictures as an old bent woman bending over a cauldron—is the mistress of the lunar current and the keeper of the secrets of Druid initiation. Imagine her as an old woman with gray hair, clad in garments of red, white, and black, stirring a steaming cauldron.

Coel

The god of the life force, Coel is the earthly manifestation of Celi, and has the additional role of god of wild animals and all wilderness places. The fragmentary nursery rhyme about "Old King Cole" seems to be a last dim scrap of folk memory of this god, possibly filtered through stories of a sixth-century British king named for him. Imagine him as a massively built man with wild hair and beard, dressed as a huntsman in russet and dark brown, with stag's antlers rising from his forehead.

Elen

The young goddess of dawn and springtime, Elen is also associated with the dragon currents that flow through the Earth and the old straight tracks that channel them. Her legends appear to be filtered through stories about a British princess of the fourth century. She is also known as Niwalen in her role as goddess of springtime greenery. Imagine her as a maiden with golden hair, clad in a short white tunic, her arms and legs bare, dancing in the forest.

Esus

The chief of tree spirits and guardian of the forests, Esus derives his name ("lord" in Old Brythonic) from an old Gaulish god, but his role in Druidry seems to have been a result of nineteenth- and twentieth-century Druid visionaries. He sits in the first fork of the sacred oak and teaches the lore of trees to those who seek him out. Imagine him as a man of indeterminate age seated in a tree, dressed in brown and green garments that look like bark and leaves. His hands are long, brown, and strong as roots, and his eyes are very bright.

Hesus

Another name for Esus, containing the initial *H* of Hu and representing Esus as the protector and teacher of Druids.

Hu

The firstborn of Ced and Celi, Hu Gadarn (Hu the Mighty) is the great Druid god, the master of the element of spirit in all its forms. He is the owner of two even mightier oxen, the "two calves of the Spotted Cow"; the "spotted cow" is the night sky spotted with stars, and the two calves are the two equinoxes that trudge implacably around the circle of heaven, driving the turning mill of time. Imagine him as a mature man of immense strength with the horns of an ox curving up from his broad forehead. His hair and beard are black, he wears a robe of sky blue and a cloak as black as midnight, and light streams from him.

Niwalen

Another name for Elen as goddess of springtime greenery.

Og

Another name for Beli as god of the year.

Sul

The daughter of the Sun god Beli, Sul is the goddess of the threefold fire—the solar fire, the Sun; the telluric fire, the heat within the Earth that warms healing hot springs; and the common fire that blazes on every hearth. She is the mistress of healing and of all domestic crafts. See her as an adult woman with golden hair, wearing a white gown, red cloak, and ornaments of gold.

BIBLIOGRAPHY

Agrippa, Henry Cornelius. *Three Books of Occult Philosophy* (St. Paul, MN: Llewellyn, 1993).

Arbatel of Magick, in Henry Cornelius Agrippa. *Fourth Book of Occult Philosophy* (Kila, MT: Kessinger, 1992).

Ashe, Geoffrey. *Mythology of the British Isles* (London: Methuen, 1990).

Berman, Morris. *The Reenchantment of the World* (New York: Bantam, 1981).

Butler, E. M. *Ritual Magic* (New York: Noonday, 1959).

Butler, W. E. *The Magician: His Training and Work* (North Hollywood, CA: Wilshire, 1959).

Butterworth, E. A. S. *The Tree at the Navel of the Earth* (Berlin: De Gruyter, 1970).

Carr-Gomm, Philip. *The Druid Way* (Shaftesbury, Dorset: Element, 1993).

————. *What Do Druids Believe?* (London: Granta, 2006).

Carr-Gomm, Philip, and Stephanie Carr-Gomm. *The Druid Animal Oracle* (NY: Fireside Books, 1994).

————. *The Druid Craft Tarot* (NY: St. Martin's Press, 2005).

————. *The Druid Planet Oracle* (NY: St. Martin's Press, 2008).

Crowley, Aleister. *Magick in Theory and Practice* (New York: Dover, 1976).

Evans-Wentz, W. Y. *The Fairy-Faith in Celtic Countries* (New York: Citadel, 1966).

Gantz, Jeffrey, trans. *The Mabinogion* (London: Penguin, 1976).

Gardner, Adelaide. M*editation: A Practical Study* (Wheaton, IL: Quest, 1968).

Geoffrey of Monmouth. *The History of the Kings of Britain* (London: Penguin, 1966).

Graves, Robert. *TheWhite Goddess* (NewYork: Farrar, Strauss and Giroux, 1966).

Graves, Tom. *Needles of Stone Revisited* (Glastonbury: Gothic Image, 1986).

Gray, William G. *Magical Ritual Methods* (York Beach, ME: Weiser, 1980).

———. *Western Inner Workings* (York Beach, ME: Weiser, 1983).

Greer, John Michael. *The Druidry Handbook* (San Francisco, CA: Weiser, 2006).

———. *The Natural Magic Encyclopedia* (St. Paul, MN: Llewellyn, 2000).

Hall, Manly Palmer. *Self-Unfoldment by Disciplines of Realization* (Los Angeles: Philosophical Research Society, 1942).

Ingerman, Sandra. *Medicine for the Earth* (New York: Three Rivers, 2000).

Knight, Gareth. *Occult Exercises and Practices* (Albuquerque, NM: Sun Chalice, 1998).

———. *The Secret Tradition in Arthurian Legend* (York Beach, ME: Weiser, 1996).

Laurie, Erynn R. "The Cauldron of Poesy," *Obsidian 2* (Spring 1996), pp. 23–30.

Lévi, Eliphas. *Transcendental Magic* (San Francisco, CA: Weiser, 1972).

McLean, Adam. *The Magical Calendar* (Grand Rapids, MI: Phanes, 1994).

Michell, John. *The View over Atlantis* (New York: Ballantine, 1969).

Mountfort, Paul Rhys. *Ogam: The Celtic Oracle of the Trees* (Rochester, VT: Destiny, 2002).

Murray, Colin, and Liz Murray. *The Celtic Tree Oracle* (New York: St. Martins Press, 1988).

Neihardt, John, ed. *Black Elk Speaks* (Lincoln, NB: University of Nebraska Press, 1988).

Regardie, Israel. *The Golden Dawn* (St. Paul, MN: Llewellyn, 1971).

Robertson, Colin. *The Druidic Order of the Pendragon* (Loughborough, Leics: Thoth, 2004).

Robinson, James M., ed. *The Nag Hammadi Library* (San Francisco: HarperSanFrancisco, 1988).

Roszak, Theodore. *The Voice of the Earth* (New York: Touchstone, 1992).

———. *Where the Wasteland Ends* (Garden City, NY: Doubleday, 1972).

Sadhu, Mouni. *Concentration: A Guide to Mental Mastery* (North Hollywood, CA: Wilshire, 1959).

———. *Meditation: An Outline for Practical Study* (North Hollywood, CA: Wilshire, 1967).

Smiles, Sam. *The Image of Antiquity: Ancient Britain and the Romantic Imagination* (New Haven, CT: Yale University Press, 1994).

Stewart, R. J. *The Prophetic Vision of Merlin* (London: Arkana, 1986).

———. *The Way of Merlin* (London: Aquarian, 1991).

Tolstoy, Nikolai. *The Quest for Merlin* (Boston: Little, Brown, and Co., 1985).

Tompkins, Peter, and Christopher Bird. *Secrets of the Soil* (Anchorage, AK: Earthpulse, 1998).

White, Lynn, Jr. "The Historical Roots of Our Ecological Crisis," *Science,* March 10, 1967, pp. 1203–07.

Williams ab Ithel, J., ed. *The Barddas of Iolo Morganwg* (San Francisco, CA: Weiser, 2004).

Wood, Ernest. *Concentration: An Approach to Meditation* (Wheaton, IL: Quest, 1949).

Yeats, W. B. *A Vision and Related Writings,* edited by A. Norman Jeffares (London: Arena, 1990).

INDEX

ABOUT THE AUTHOR

John Michael Greer is the Grand Archdruid of the Ancient Order of Druids in America and a widely respected writer and teacher. He has been a student of the occult traditions and nature spirituality for more than twenty-five years. He began following the Druid path in 1993 with initiation into the Order of Bards, Ovates, and Druids, where he has been honored with awards and elected offices. Greer is the author of numerous articles and books, including *The Druidry Handbook* (Weiser, 2006), and he is co-author of *Pagan Prayer Beads* (Weiser, 2007) and *Learning Ritual Magic* (Weiser, 2004). Greer lives in Ashland, Oregon, with his wife where he can be found blogging at *http://www.thearchdruidreport.com.*

© Patrick Claflin

TO OUR READERS

Weiser Books, an imprint of Red Wheel/Weiser, publishes books across the entire spectrum of occult and esoteric subjects. Our mission is to publish quality books that will make a difference in people's lives without advocating any one particular path or field of study. We value the integrity, originality, and depth of knowledge of our authors.

Our readers are our most important resource, and we appreciate your input, suggestions, and ideas about what you would like to see published. Please feel free to contact us, to request our latest book catalog, or to be added to our mailing list.

Red Wheel/Weiser, LLC
500 Third Street, Suite 230
San Francisco, CA 94107
www.redwheelweiser.com